A SMALL BUSINESS OWNERS GUIDEBOOK

A survival guide for South African Small Business Owners

Vic Soffiantini

Italic Publishers, Durban, South Africa

Published by:

    Italic Publishers

    P.O. Box 4618

    Durban 4000

    South Africa

Cover design by: VAS

Illustrations by Microsoft Office.com

First Edition 2009

Second Edition 2010

Third Edition 2011

Fourth Edition 2013

Fifth Edition 2018 with corrections

Printed and Bound by: Lulu.com

Sales orders at: http://www.lulu.com

ISBN 978-1-4461-6737-3

I dedicate this book to my wife Cynthia, my two daughters, Jeanette and Jacqueline, and my four grandchildren. If it was not for their encouragement, I would not have had the inspiration and perspiration to write this book based on over 40 years of the good and the bad business experiences.

For any errors noted or suggestions, please send an email message to vasmweb@yahoo.com

Contents

Preface

This South African survival guide booklet has been written for those entrepreneurs who are about to start, or who have just started their own small businesses and are still "learning the ropes"; also for those owners/directors' whose companies are struggling to survive and need some new straight business solutions.

Many aspects of the book are also applicable to businesses in other developed or developing countries.

The author, a graduate in Business Economics, is a Director of Companies and has attempted to write this booklet in plain understandable English, without any fanciful words or complex "number crunching" accounting calculations.

There are also many principles included in this book which will help you, the reader, not only to succeed in business but also to live a more rewarding lifestyle.

You do not need a college or university degree to start or run your own business; just some common sense and a helping hand from an experienced business person!

There is some repetition in this book, but these parts are important and thus have to be remembered.

If your business has been going for more than five years, then you can safely assume that you are in for the long term, but do not become complacent; because *"if you snooze you lose"*, this basically means to be awake to all and any opportunities that may still come your way.

It has been stated by many business gurus that 80% of small businesses fail within the first two years, BUT you could be that 20% that become a major success!

This manual will help you to be part of that 20% of small business owners who pass the first two years and continue to be successful.

This 80:20 ratio is known as the *Pareto Principle* (aka *80/20 Rule)* and can be sensibly applied to almost anything; for example you could find out that 80% of your income (the most **effect** of anything) is only coming from 20% of your customers (the least of the **cause**)!

BEE requirements and any aspect or laws related thereto, will not be discussed in this book as this broad field is forever changing. It is recommended that you check with your attorney or your local Chamber of Commerce about the latest legal requirements. Basically BEE regulations in South Africa mandate and control equal employment opportunities and the procurement of supplies Most other developed countries have similar laws.

However, you must register on the National B-BBEE Registry with the Department of Trade and Industry, irrespective of how small or large your business, as you will be required to state your BEE level or status when tendering for work or applying for loans; or even buying/ordering goods and services from your suppliers.

Many large corporations require you to be evaluated (most probably based on your BEE status) by them as a "Preferred" supplier of goods or services, before they will award you any tenders or work; i.e. you must fulfil certain criteria before being listed on their supplier database.

"Drive thy business or it will drive thee"----------*quote from Benjamin Franklin*

Introduction

There are many regular pitfalls when operating a small business in South Africa or in any other capitalistic country. An astute business owner will be aware of the many possible obstacles in trying to achieve the objective of any business, **i.e. to make a profit (namely, The Economic Motive of a business).**

One of the major financial problems in running a small business is that every outside person or organisation that is connected to your business in some way or other, **are out to get money from you, so beware!**

In business there is no such thing as a "free lunch"; your associates, suppliers, service providers, accountants, insurance brokers, attorneys, etc. are also out to make money (i.e. to make a profit for their own businesses) from **you** (the economic motive).

You must have perseverance when things go wrong and they will, but you will overcome these obstacles. Experience is the best teacher.

You must LOVE what you are doing in order for your business to succeed.

Your determination and your passion for your business will help you to succeed.

The enjoyment and satisfaction of managing and controlling your own destiny is what owning your own business is all about.

It is a 24/7 hobby that YOU have chosen. Also, in order to succeed you must have integrity and be committed to conduct trustingly an open and ethical business relationship with all your staff, suppliers of goods and services, public servants, customers or clients, and all those that come in contact with your business. Remember that the other person on the end of that telephone line, "tweet" or "sms" message, is also a person; or that organisation's email address you are writing to, is actually a person who is reading your email as a representative of that organization.

Also, you must be diligent at all times when making any financial or contractual decisions, whether in writing or otherwise. *Due diligence* in all matters is always worth the time and trouble.

Ask your potential customers what they want and then give it to them at a price that they are willing to pay.

Basically, in any business, according to Marcus Lemonis of the TV series 'The Profit'', there are only 6 things that a business owner needs to concentrate on:

People (your employees, customers, suppliers); process (your operation or manufacturing of goods), product (what you selling) and of course *profit* (what you take home!

> *A business cannot cause itself to go bankrupt.......................it is people that cause businesses to fail!*

"*The use of money is all the advantage of having money*"
----------*quote from Benjamin Franklin*

Chapter 1

Advantages and Disadvantages

Some advantages of having your own business

- Your time is your own;

- You control your own work schedule;

- You make all the decisions, promotions and get to make that famous boss expression "you're fired!" But beware! There could be legal implications of any decision that you may make on the spur of the moment;

- There is no corporate back-stabbing or obsessions with climbing the corporate ladder; or disagreements with bosses or corporate colleagues;

- **You** control how much money you make or lose (this might be a disadvantage to some owners who are inherently unable to control the flow of cash --- **the most important aspect of any business);**

- You decide your salary structure or drawings;

- If you have been self-employed (i.e. own your business) for more than 5 years, then it is easy to get superior personal and business credit deals; you are considered now low risk;

- Also, you should qualify for lower insurance premiums; if you combine policies;

- Gain a respected status in your business community;

- Some sundry personal household expenses may legally be paid out of the business funds, as trading expenses, e.g. stationery, home phone and internet expenses, travel and entertainment;

but first seek advice from your bookkeeper or accountant.

Some disadvantages of having your own business

- You are always on duty 24/7/365;

- You can never take a long pre-planned holiday, unless you are lucky in having a reliable and honest manager or business partner;

- You can never get sick or be hospitalised, or even have an accident;

- You should ethically pay your staff first and then yourself; but sometimes there might not be enough cash in bank, so staff and landlord (your rent) have to be paid first;

- You are continuously under stress; however some people thrive on stress;

- Note that in most cases, the bigger your business, the bigger are your headaches! even if you do delegate some of your managerial duties to your staff; however, the final responsibility always remains yours..............do not be greedy, otherwise you will fall *hard*;

- At the end of the day, it is YOU who is accountable, legally and ethically, for the actions of your staff and your business dealings;

- Disrupts family life; here you need the full support, cooperation and understanding of all close members of your family and friends.

"Effort only fully releases its reward after a person refuses to quit"

----------*quote from Napoleon Hill*

NOTES:

Suggest you list here YOUR advantages and disadvantages:

Chapter 2

Legal Entities of Businesses

What is a Legal Entity?

A legal entity is basically a trust, person or an organization that can represent itself in all forms of legal contracts.

The first step in starting a business is to reserve a name at CIPC. Here you can also register your copyrights, designs, patents and trademarks.

All businesses (except sole proprieties) in South Africa, have to register with the "Companies and Intellectual Property Commission office (CIPC)" at www.cipc.co.za.

"Companies not for gain"

Are commonly referred to as Section 21 companies, they are generally some type of charitable organisation.

Public Limited Companies (Ltd):

Are those companies of large organizations (share capital of over R25 million) whose shares are listed on a Stock Exchange (in South Africa it is the JSE) and can be bought or sold by any legal person; the company must have at least 2 directors and at least 7 shareholders. Its financial liabilities are limited according to the Companies Act and its amendments.

You may operate your small business under any one of the legal entities below:

An ALTX Public Limited Companies (Ltd):

Small and medium-sized enterprises (SMEs) who have more than a R2 million share capital; whose shares are listed on a Stock Exchange (in South Africa it is the JSE) and can be bought or sold by any legal person.

Proprietary Limited Companies (Pty) Ltd:

These are the companies of mostly small and medium-sized enterprises (SMEs) whose shares cannot be bought or sold publicly on a Stock Exchange, but may be *sold* privately. Its shareholders/owners' liabilities are somewhat limited.

A Memorandum of Association of the company must accompany the application for registration. These private companies may not have more than 50 shareholders.

Partnerships:

These are those businesses that are owned and probably managed by two or more persons, but limited to twenty partners.

It is advisable to register the name of a partnership; and get a lawyer to draw up a Contract of Partnership between all the partners. It is also advisable to take out a life insurance policy of each partner.

These businesses are usually professional type, such as dental or medical practices.

Sole Proprietorship:

These are those businesses that are owned and probably managed by one person (yourself).

It is advisable to register the name of the business, even if you are the only person running the business. The name of a business (also its website domain name) could have substantial financial value in the future, e.g. its goodwill and also if it has a much sought-after domain name on the internet. Refer to Chapter 7. This could be your "Trading Name". Note that a Trading Name and a company registered name could be two different things. A Trading Name is not mandatory. You must list and register both. Also suggest you register a shortened name that describes your type of business.

Franchises:

Basically, this is where you buy the right to operate a certain business (from a franchisor) under a certain brand name where the franchisor tells you what to do, how to do it, when to do it and at what price to sell to your customers. In return, he/she is supposed to do the entire advertising, bulk buying, training, etc.; but you have to pay him/her regular royalties from the proceeds of your business, plus various other commissions.

In other words it is your business, but *you are working for someone else*; however, there are advantages to this type of business, such as assistance with staff training, administration, promotions, advertising, etc.

More information can be obtained from the Franchise Association of South Africa at http://www.fasa.co.za/

Or at the following websites:

http://www.whichfranchise.co.za

http://www.franchisezone.co.za

http://www.safranchisewarehouse.co.za/

http://www.franchisefinder.co.za/

Or "Google" it on the internet at: www.google.com

Alternatively, if you are brave enough, you can start your own franchise (franchisor) and sell your brand to franchisees.

"Success is not final, failure is not fatal; it is the courage to continue that counts"

----------quote from Winston Churchill

NOTES:

Suggest you list here the possible legal entities for YOUR business:

Chapter 3

Legal Requirements of a business

A small business is generally defined as any business that has less than 50 employees and an annual turnover of less than R5 million.

The following are some of the legal obligations and government acts, applicable to certain types of businesses in South Africa:

- Basic Conditions of Employment Act 75 of 1997 (a very important Act)
- Broad-Based Black Economic Employment Act
- Companies and Intellectual Property Commission, CIPC (for registration and annual renewal of businesses, etc.); refer to www.cipc.co.za (a very important Act)
- New Companies Act (Act 71 of 2008) (a very important Act)
- Competitions Act
- Compensation for Occupational Injuries and Diseases Act 130 of 1993 (a very crucial Act---Compensation Fund--- for reporting injuries that occurred at the work place or on site, IOD)
- Construction Industry Development Board Act
- Consumer Protection Act (Act 68 of 2008), CPA, (a very important Act)

- Copyright Act & Trademarks (Trade Marks division of CIPC)

- Counterfeit Goods Act

- Currency and Exchanges Act

- Customs and Excise Act

- Designs Act

- Employment Equity Act (important today w.r.t. sexual harassment complaints)

- Engineering Professions Act

- Environment Conservation Act

- Estate Agency Affairs Act

- Fertilizers, Farm Feeds, Agricultural Remedies and Stock Remedies Act

- Finance Act

- Foodstuffs, Cosmetics and Disinfectants Act

- Health Professions Act

- Income Tax Act (a very important Act)

- Marketing Agricultural Products Act

- Measuring Units & Measurement Standards Act 18 of 2006

- Merchandise Marks Act

- National Advisory Council on Innovation Act

- National Credit Act 34 of 2005; (NCA)

- National Environmental Management Act

- Natural Scientific Professions Act of 2003

- National Small Business Act no. 102 of 1996

- Occupational Health & Safety Act 85 of 1993; (OHSA)

- Prescription Act 68 of 1969

- Promotion of Equality & Prevention of Unfair Discrimination Act (Pepuda);

- Promotion of Access to Information Act 2 of 2000 (PAIA)

- Protection of Personal Information Act, 2013 (POPI);

- Standards Act

- Skills Development Act

- South African Revenue Service (SARS) (for all types of taxes and customs & excise)

- Trade Practice Act

- Unfair Business Practices Act

- Unemployment Insurance Act 30 of 1966; (UIF)

- Unemployment Insurance Contributions Act

Also note their current Amendments and Government Notices, as well as your local Bye-Laws.

The Companies Act regulates most South African companies. This Act and the Companies and Intellectual Property Commission (CIPC) administers initial and annual registration of businesses, also offers free advice on patents.

No matter what legal entity/type of business you are involved with, you still have to be personally registered as a (Provisional) taxpayer. Also your business must be registered as a company taxpayer if it is a type of (Pty) Ltd. However, if you are classed as a "Small Business" then the company tax rate is lower than that of medium or larger companies.

All businesses with more than one employee (i.e. you as owner plus if you employ one or more persons) you must register as an "Employer" with SARS (the taxman!) as well as with the Unemployment Insurance

Act (UIF) and the Skills Development Act. Also register as a VAT vendor with SARS.

Make sure that you receive registration numbers from these government departments.

For any business that has more than 50 employees, an "Affirmative Action Policy" has to be complied with and registered.

Plus, any local municipal requirements such as business licenses (e.g. businesses that deal in food, liquor and/or entertainment).

Note that the labour laws in South Africa can be a minefield to negotiate, suggest you immediately consult a registered labour consultant as soon as you foresee or anticipate any staff problems. Advice may also be obtained from some local websites; also you can subscribe to some labour advisory businesses, or get assistance from your local Chamber of Commerce.

For further government bills and other documentation, refer to their website at:

http://www.search.gov.za/info/advancedSearch.jsp

All businesses are supposed to display the following posters on their premises, in such an area that they are visible and accessible to all staff:

Basic Conditions of Employment Act;

Summary Employment Equity Act;

Occupational Health and Safety Act;

Important Notice Duties of Every Employee at Work.

NOTES:

Suggest you list here the legal requirements and other issues for YOUR business:

Chapter 4

Basic Business Criteria

If you have technical skills, you should be in a technical type business; but first you must learn some basic business skills otherwise you will not succeed. For example, you might be the best welder in the world, but if you do not know how to handle cash flow, interpret contracts, check bank statements, operate within a budget, and control employees, you will probably not succeed as a successful AND wealthy business man. Note that your business might be successful, but you could not be making money for yourself.................you should always make sure that you pay yourself 10% of your earnings before you pay anyone else. There are four important economic criteria that a business owner or entrepreneur must follow:

1. The economic motive................i.e. make a profit;

2. The Supply and Demand curve............i.e. can you supply the demand of the market?

3. The Supply and Demand curve..............i.e. is there a demand for your supplies/services, now and in the future?

4. The Supply and Demand curve ....when there is a high demand in the market place, for goods and services similar to yours, then the selling price can increase; but when there is a decrease in the demand for your goods or services, then you

have to lower your prices, or diversify into another segment of the marketplace using your resources you have on hand.

There are also basically only 13 recognised reasons that will assist you in establishing success in business as well as in your general life.

1. You must keep at least <u>10% of all your earnings</u> just for yourself (why not! it is your money!); i.e. before you pay anyone you pay yourself regularly 10% of all your earnings.

2. You must <u>work productively</u> in order to achieve goal 1 above. If you can dream about it, and you have the determination, then you can make <u>IT HAPPEN</u>;

3. Take calculated risks; but be wise as this astuteness only comes from bad experiences. Apply a little caution (diligent). Remember that men/women of action are favoured by the Goddess of Good Luck.

4. You must <u>control your expenses</u>, i.e. operate within a budget; regularly checking that you do NOT spend more than you earn (make sure that your assets (what you got) are greater in value, after depreciation, than your liabilities (what you owe out).

5. Make "<u>your money" multiply</u>; i.e. your savings (from 1 above) and business profits, invested in a bank financial product that will yield you COMPOUND interest (i.e. interest earned on interest already earned). Compound interest is a very powerful tool for "growing" money!

6. <u>Protect your assets</u> by insuring what you have; make sure you have adequate insurance for all contingencies (loss of earnings, your life, car, etc.). Refer to Chapter 16.

7. <u>Purchase your premises</u> or home. Property, if purchased wisely, is one of the best investments. Refer to Chapter 7 below.

8. Make adequate <u>provision for your future</u> (retirement).

9. <u>Continuously educate</u> yourself and keep up to date with current events in your particular field of expertise or career. This increases your ability to earn more money.

10. Beware! <u>Everybody</u> is out to take your hard earned money away from you…….. your accountant, your attorney, your insurance broker, your banker, your supplier and even your customers (customers want the best deal available)!

You have been warned.

11. However, you must remember that these people/associates/colleagues/etc. above, also have to make money, but let them make their money from someone else.

12. Note that it is people/staff/you that makes or breaks a business! A company cannot collapse on its own……….it is people that cause it to collapse!

13. In business, if your business has many competitors, then you must offer a more competitive product/service. <u>Do not enter</u> into a price war with your competition as you are likely to go BUST quicker than them! "Go the extra mile" by offering extras such as free delivery, discounts, coupons, etc.

Contracts:

This might be one of the scariest areas of running your own business!

There will be many occasions when you will have to deal with contracts; these are mostly written agreements between two persons or organisations such as buying an insurance policy, placing an order for capital/major equipment, signing a rental agreement, employing staff, etc.

If your business owns or has some sensitive information, you will need to protect it by having your senior staff sign a "Restraint of Trade" contract. Here you have to legally stipulate a fixed time period, say 3 years after termination of employment and a restrictive location, say within a 50km radius of your business. You do not want your top staff resigning and taking with them your customers, trade secrets, formulations or any other company information or other intellectual property.

A contract is a legally binding agreement between two parties. This agreement should be reasonable and fair to both parties. If the contract is unreasonable and heavily biased towards one party, then it is possible to dispute its validity in a court of law.

When purchasing or leasing machinery try to avoid signing contracts that have a "surety clause". This clause basically means that if your business cannot pay, then you personally have to pay the account, even if you have to sell your home. *Actually if you sign a contract containing this clause, then you are signing away your rights to your own money!*

When suppliers stipulate that this is a clause in their standard contract, then try another supplier who will not insist on this clause. The surety clause is a very dangerous one when it is applied to you as a buyer of goods or services. However, if you have a contract with your customers (i.e. people you are selling goods to) or clients (i.e. people you are selling a service to) then you must have this clause in your contract with them to safeguard yourself.

In any supplier or contractor's contract you must read and understand the fine print as well as the main text. If in doubt, seek legal advice.

In disputing contracts, the courts will take, *inter alia*, the following into consideration:

- What are the facts?

- What was the real intention of the writer of the contract?

- Is the contract reasonable to both parties?

- Is there a time period involved, or is the contract a perpetual contract?

- Has the contract been notarised and signed by both parties in the presence of witnesses?

- Contracts should preferably be completed and signed in black pen. Each page should be initialled by all parties to the contract.

Contract documentation is available at

http://www.agreementsonline.co.za

Loans:

When applying for a business loan from a bank or micro lender, do not disclose all your financial resources (such as your second savings account, or stock shares, etc.) as collateral. Disclose only the barest minimum requirement to them. This will give you some sort of a safety net if something goes wrong with the loan.

Keep your personal bank account separate from your business bank account; that is place your business account with a different bank. The reason for this is that mistakes can be made by bank clerks, electronic communications, computerisation of records, etc. and you do not want both accounts frozen for any reason whatsoever.

It is unwise to use second mortgage on your home as a business loan, rather take out a personal loan with another bank or institution and get someone to sign as surety, or use a Life Insurance policy as collateral (i.e. you cede the policy over to the bank; this means that should something happen to you, the bank collects its share first before your estate……..but remember that once you have paid off the loan, request the bank to immediately cancel the cession and return the documents to you).

You can also apply to your insurance company for a loan on your life insurance policy. They might grant you a short loan of about 90% of what you have paid into the policy.

"He who waits upon fortune is never sure of dinner"

----------quote from Benjamin Franklin

NOTES:

Suggest you list here your important aspects of YOUR business:

Chapter 5

Business Plan

How to compile a comprehensive "business plan" in detail will **not** be discussed here, only the basics. Many other aspects stated here are also applicable to those starting, or purchasing, a business for the first time. There are many books and other publications available on how to compile a "business plan". Also there is a great deal of information on the internet.

A simple "business plan" may be defined or described as the orderly compilation of:

- the name of your business (to be registered); e.g. *Sally Holdings (Pty) Ltd*, trading as *Sally's Belts 4 Us*;

- what to manufacture or sell (e.g. belts); or alternatively what service to provide (e.g. insurance broker, pathologist);

- what resources are needed (e.g. capital funding for machinery, start-up loans, staff, premises, accountant);

- to whom to sell your product or service (i.e. your market, e.g. general public, wholesalers, hospitals);

- where to manufacture or sell your product or service (i.e. your location, e.g. factory, shop, pathology laboratory);

- your plan on how to sell or promote your product or service (e.g. passing trade in shopping mall, social media on internet, websites, radio and TV, agents);

- compile a list of your legal requirements pertaining to your type of business (city health regulations, business licences, registration as an employer, VAT vendor registration);

- who are your main competitors (from your market research results; e.g. another belt shop in same suburb, national or international companies providing similar products or services);

- why customers should come to you and not go to your competition; i.e. what advantage do you plan to have over your competitors;

- your sources of capital funding;

- how to cost it (**your budget**);

- and calculate your **estimated profit** at the end of the day (this is also part of your budget).

Basically it is the survey results or reports on your market research that you have done, as well as any strategic planning that you have undertaken. Normally banks, shareholders and prospective partners request a business plan from you before they make any decisions.

A comprehensible business plan can be used as part of your company or business internal Standard Operating Procedures (SOP). These SOP's should be in place in any business, especially those that require accreditation (e.g. ISO 9000) or external auditing (e.g. HACCP).

Your business plan can be the basis for your Mission Statement

An SOP basically tells you and your staff:

- what to do;

- how to do it (e.g. what machinery to use);

- when to do it (e.g. when to order new stock,; use the "Just-in-Time" (JIT) principle; i.e. order new stock only when the amount on hand has dropped to the predetermined level;

- a contingency plan as to what to do when something goes wrong (e.g. customer complaints or a customer care hotline).

Thus, your Business Plan, Mission Statement and Standard Operating Procedures should deliver a consistent image and value to your customers.

A business plan must include a Mission Statement; this can be a simple one page document outlining basically your aim or what you do for your customers.

Also a "Health and Safety" policy should be compiled.

Suitable formats can be downloaded from the internet; just *Google* the word "free business formats ".

There are also many so-called consultants who can assist you in compiling a business plan. However, the only person who really knows what you want to do is you!

"A person who never made a mistake never tried anything new"

----------*quote from Albert Einstein*

NOTES:

Suggest you sketch a rough business plan, or your future plans here for YOUR business:

Chapter 6

Business Name

What is a Business Name?

The name of your business is very important. It should describe what your business is all about, e.g. "Belts for Us" is a suitable descriptive name for a business that makes and/or sells belts. This is also important for a domain name when you have your own website for your business on the internet, e.g. www.BeltsforUs.co.za and hence your email address would be easy to remember, such as beltsforus@gmail.co.za. Your email address should preferably be something like info@beltsforus.com.

You must check on the internet if your proposed name has not already been used by someone else; check at www.whois.com

Another important aspect of the name is the very first letter of the name. This letter should preferably start with the letter "a" so that your business is listed alphabetically at the top of any business directories such as the telephone Yellow Pages, other printed trade directories and sometimes those online directories on the internet.

Legally your name must not be the same or cause confusion with other businesses with similar names, e.g. "BeltsForU". Note that if your business is a (Pty) Ltd registered company, then the name would somewhat be automatically protected. However, you may reserve the name through the Department of Trade & Industry (DTI), at Companies and Intellectual Property Commission (CIPC). Your business name should not only be descriptive but also short and easy to remember. The name should also contain one or more keywords that your potential customers would search for on the internet (e.g. belts).

A shortened version of your business name, and/or trading name if different from your registered business name, may also be registered with CIPC.

You may also register a translated name, e.g. if your business name is in an African language, you may register the English translation. Also check that there are no adverse meanings, or interpretation, to your name if it is translated into another language.

If you have a website, you must keep your registration of your Domain Name up-to-date. Registration is usually annually with your ISP (Internet Service Provider).

"Just because something doesn't do what you planned it to do doesn't mean it's useless"

----------quote from Thomas A Edison

NOTES:

Suggest you list here the some possible names or future names for YOUR business:

Chapter 7

Location of business premises

The most important aspect of any business is location, location, location!

What is Location?

This is where your business premises are located geographically; that is, the address from which you operate.

It is very critical that you are in the right location. Of course, this is not critical if you are operating an online or internet business from home, but here you must ensure that you are catering to the regions or countries that you want to do business.

What is the right location?

The answer to this question depends upon where your customers are and what type of business you are operating.

Your business must be easily accessible to your customers. Your customers will not come to you if it is difficult for them to find your premises, or to find you on the world wide web (i.e. the internet) Conversely, your customers must be easily accessible by you......e.g. if your customer is in another city or another country.......of course this does not apply if you are operating a national or international business.

If you are a shop selling general goods to the public, then you need to be near shopping centres or other areas where there is *"passing trade"*. That is, you want to be where people (potential customers) have to walk past your shop or can see your signs or shop.

If you are providing a service, e.g. TV repairs, then you must position your premises in an area that has a large number of TV users, so that you spend minimum time travelling to and from the customers' houses.

If you provide an engineering service to the shipping industry, then you must locate near a harbour.

Get the idea?

Premises-----Rent or buy?

The answer to this question depends upon what type of business you are operating.

Commercial properties are, in general, more stable as an investment then residential properties.

Recommend you buy your premises, if finances are available. You do not want to waste your hard-earned money on paying off someone else's (landlord) mortgage bond; whereas you could use this rent money to pay off your own commercial bond. Strongly recommend that you do not put your personal name on the bond, but that of your business name or a trust. Get advice from your accountant or attorney about tax implications.

You do not want the bondholder (bank) to come and take (foreclosure) your own home and personal assets, if your business should fail.........but do not worry, because if you follow the advice given in this book, you are sure to succeed and make lots of money.

However, it is recommended that you rent first for the first two or three years, to make sure that you have your business in the right locality. Refer to Strategic Planning, Chapter 15.

But be careful, the area that you are operating in, could change virtually overnight........how acceptable are your present and future business neighbours, or what plans does the local municipality have for your area?

Note that if you rent a shop in a shopping mall, you will also have to pay over to the managing agents or landlord a percentage of your turnover, in addition to the rent! Also be aware of escalation clauses in your rent/lease agreement/contract, these could be as high as 20%.

Rent payments are one of the biggest killers of small businesses, second is greedy owners who fleece their own business by taking out excessive amounts of cash either as a high salary or drawings!

If you are going to rent premises, then ensure that you are aware of the amount of floor space that you physically require. The landlord will advertise a rental cost per square area (metres or feet). However, there are two basic ways of stating the floor area for rentals: the GLA (Gross Leasable Area) is that area which includes *the pro rata* of any exclusive use sections such as stairs, passages and communal toilets in the building; this is usually the total area. The GFA (Gross Floor Area) is that portion that you can physically use. This figure is a lot less than the GLA. However, the rent that you are charged would be that based on the GLA.

"Let no feeling of discouragement prey upon you, and in the end you are sure to succeed"

----------*quote from Abraham Lincoln*

NOTES:

Suggest you list here location requirements for YOUR business:

Chapter 8

Bookkeeping and Accounting

What is Bookkeeping?

Bookkeeping is the process of recording or entering financial figures (e.g. from invoices, statements, debit notes, etc.) in an orderly fashion, such as debits and credits, into "books of account" or computer software programmes; up to the "Trial Balance" stage, but before any quarterly or annual adjustments (journal entries) have been made. A Trial Balance is just a list of all credits (money in) and a list of all debits (money out).

It is based on the double-entry system, i.e. for every debit entry into a ledger account there must be a corresponding credit entry of same amount; thus the "Trial Balance" must *balance*.

For example:

> when paying out, you *debit* the expense or supplier ledger account and *credit* your bank account or Cash Book;

> when receiving money (income, interest received, etc.) you *credit* your income account and *debit* your bank account or Cash Book.

Debit entries are, by convention, on the left side of the ledger account and credits are on the right side of the ledger account.

Tax invoices:

A *tax invoice* is a non-negotiable numbered document (i.e. bill of sale or contract of sale) issued by a seller (e.g. you) to a buyer (e.g. your customer), which states the date of sale or service, identifies full names, addresses and contact details of both parties, quantifies the items or services sold, displays VAT registration numbers of both parties, shows detailed prices and discounts (if any).

Always show on your invoices a "Payment due date".

Vat Output is the amount of vat that you add onto your sales price/invoice to charge to your customers. This amount less your Vat Input, is paid by you, to the taxman (SARS).

Vat Input is the vat charged by your suppliers on the goods/services that you have purchased. This is the vat that you claim back from the taxman; in reality you just deduct it from your output vat.

There are 3 types of vat charges that you must choose from to put in your invoice to your customers:

Standard-rated supplies (at 14%) is the most common rate to charge;

Exempt supplies applies to certain goods or services only (check with your accountant);

Zero-rated supplies applies to certain foodstuffs and export sales (but check with your accountant).

The invoice document should refer back to Delivery Notes, where applicable.

Always submit your invoices or Debit Notes immediately after goods or services have been rendered to your customers or clients. The sooner you submit these documents (online) to your customers, the sooner you will get paid!

Other documents:

A *Delivery Note* is a non-negotiable numbered document issued by a seller to a buyer, which states the mode and date of delivery of goods sold, identifies full names, addresses and contact details of both parties, identifies and quantifies the items sold. The seller's conditions and terms of his/her business are also stated thereon. Usually, it is a requirement of the seller that the buyer signs this document on receipt of goods stating that the goods were received in good condition.

A *Debit Note* is a document issued by a service provider (e.g. insurance company) or seller, stating that a prescribed amount of money will be required from the buyer before a certain date, without an actual sale being made.

A *pro-forma invoice* is a dated and numbered document issued by a seller to a buyer, which, identifies full names, addresses and contact details of both parties, quantifies the items or services to be sold, and, shows detailed prices (including delivery charges, etc.) and discounts (if any). This document is similar to a Quotation or invoice, but becomes payable before the goods or services have been delivered.

A Remittance Advice, also known as a Creditors Reconciliation statement is a document sent to you informing you which of your invoices or accounts have been paid, by your customer.

A must these days is a user-friendly computer programme for bookkeeping or financial record keeping. There are many commercial software packages available such as the generally well known ones:

- Pastel Accounting at Sage at http://www.sage.co.za
- QuickBooks Accounting at http://www.quickbooks.co.za

Some free open-source programmes, download from the internet, are:

- http://www.gnucash.org
- http://www.turbocash.net; a popular South African product.

Or, make your own spreadsheet, e.g. use Microsoft Excel.

You might also need other business software programmes or databases, such as a CRM (Customer Relationship Management tool) which is used to manage contacts from sales (past and present).

If you want to go big, then get a computerised CMS (Content Management System tool) software programme that will handle all your business data and records; or an ERP (Enterprise Resource Planning tool).

All these computerised management tools are sold on the internet or you could hire a computer programmer to code these databases to suit your exact requirements.

To employ a bookkeeper is expensive, so if your business is a non-cash type and has less than 5000 customers/clients, then do your own bookkeeping using one of the above software programmes.

The advantage here is that you can keep regular tabs on exactly how much money is coming in and what expenses are being paid out.

Many small businesses have gone bust because the owner outsourced or employed a doubtful or incompetent bookkeeper or financial manager and hence lost control of his/her business finances.

Most of these software programmes go further than just the "Trial Balance" stage and will give you reports on cash flow, outstanding debtors and even up to date profitability of your business; provided of course that all transactions have been entered correctly.

Accounting is the work done by an accountant in preparing the quarterly or annual financial statements which include the Income Statement (aka Profit & Loss Statement), Balance Sheet and Cash Flow Statement.

An external chartered accountant or auditor is the person that checks the correctness or trueness of your bookkeeping, usually for tax purposes.

Basically, in order to run financially a successful business, you need to know and watch only 3 figures:

> Sales or revenue;
> Gross Profit; and
> Net profit

A "**Trial Balance**" statement is basically just a data check to see that all the credit side of the books balance with all the debit side of the books. This is the stage at which most office bookkeepers finalise their books; however, they also do the "Bank Reconciliation Statement" i.e. check that all the entries in the monthly statement from your bank reconciles with his/her corresponding entries in your books of accounting. Thereafter all the adjustments or journal entries such as depreciation, amortisation, is done by an accountant or the company accounting officer.

Financial Statements:

1.   The most important financial record is the "**Balance Sheet.** This is like a snap photograph **at a particular date** of the financial situation of your business. It shows what your assets (what you got) are, as against your liabilities (what you owe out) and equity/capital (what money you or your partners have put into the business, including any profits or reserves). Note that your assets should be greater than your liabilities; otherwise you

will be technically "insolvent". Most accounting or bookkeeping software programmes will automatically update and calculate your Balance Sheet up to any date you require. You must study this document as it tells you what you have.

Bankruptcy is when you are legally unable to pay your debts (e.g. when your liabilities exceeds your assets by more than a factor of 2.

2. The other important financial record is the "**Income Statement**", also known as the **Trading Statement** or **Profit and Loss Statement**; this is where you calculate your profit! Basically it is a list of all income (revenue, sales) minus all expenses (operating and depreciation) to give you net earnings. Depreciation is really a non-tangible expense as it is just an assumed periodic decrease in value of capital items. The basic idea is that this monetary amount should be saved by the business (e.g. put into reserves or savings account) to cover future costs of replacing old equipment, etc. This document will also give you information as to whether there are any significant deviations in the figures when you compare it to previous periods. Thus, you can detect a problem before it becomes a disaster!

3. Another important record is your "**Cash Flow Statement**". Refer to chapter 10 below. Basically this is a record of what cash comes in and what cash goes out.....similar to a Petty Cash ledger, but of a much greater significance. **This is where a lot of businesses fail as they continually spend or borrow more than they make or are able to pay back**. This Cash Flow

statement should be checked at least monthly; against what your bank says that you have.......in other words do a "Bank Reconciliation Statement". The Balance Sheet record gives you a somewhat similar picture with respect to liquid assets (cash) but slightly distorted with figures such as "goodwill" and overvalued assets.

You need to understand the figures in your Financial Statements such as the "Income & Expenditure" and the "Balance Sheet". There are many books (and YouTube videos) on this subject of how to read and understand financial statements.

You must learn how to "**read the numbers**" in your financials to see whether your business is financially stable and growing, or unfortunately "going down the drain"!

When analysing or interpreting your Financial Statements, you should consider and calculate the following figures which will indicate to you how your business is doing:

Ratios

Where:

        "<" means "less than"

        ">" means "greater than"

Type	Equation	Recommended value
LIQUIDITY RATIO:		
Quick or Acid Test Ratio	(current assets - stock) : current liabilities	at least 1:1
Current Ratio	current assets: current liabilities	>2:1 or at least 1:1
Cash Ratio	cash : current liabilities	at least 3:1

ACTIVITY:		
Average collection period in days	accounts receivable : average sales per day	<60 if sales on credit; or 0 days for cash sales
Total assets turnover Ratio	net income : total assets	>2:1 or at least 1:1
Fixed assets turnover Ratio	net income : fixed assets	>1:1
LEVERAGE RATIOS:		
Debt Ratio	total liabilities : total assets	<0.5:1
Debt to Equity Ratio	total liabilities : total equity	<0.5:1
PROFITABILITY:		
Gross Profit	sales – cost of sales	-
% Gross Profit	$\frac{sales - cost\ of\ sales}{sales} \times 100$	>75%
% Net Profit before tax	$\frac{gross\ profit - total\ expenses}{sales} \times 100$	>30%
% Return on Assets	$\frac{net\ income}{total\ assets} \times 100$	>20%
Return on Equity Ratio (ROE)	net income : total equity	>3:1

Notes:

- Debt to Equity ratio (D:E) shows how much your business relies on borrowed money. The amount, by which your business can increase this ratio, is known as "borrowing capacity" of the business. This figure is important when applying for a bank overdraft or loans;

- Also ROE could be regarded as "Return on Investment" (ROI);

- Or, you can make any ratio you like from your financial figures in order for you to evaluate where your business is going! For example:

    $$Stock\ turnover = \frac{cost\ of\ goods\ sold}{stock\ on\ hand}$$

- Also, you can compare these ratios and other data over periods of time to see if your business is improving or on verge of doom! It is easy to compare if you plot the data on graphs (such as bar charts, pie charts) using computer spreadsheet programmes, such as Microsoft Excel.

- Balance Sheet format shows movement of capital:

Employment of Capital = Capital Employed

(money paid out = money received in)

Equations:

- **Available Capital** = current assets – current liabilities;

- **Cost of Sales** = cost of stock sold, or cost of raw materials used to manufacture product;

- **Current Assets**, aka "working capital" = cash in hand (petty cash) + bank savings and/or cheque accounts + accounts receivables (i.e. debtors, the people/customers who owe you money); this is assets that can be readily turned into cash (known as liquidity);

- **Current Liabilities** = accounts payable (i.e. creditors, the money you owe to suppliers) + sundry loans such as bank overdrafts;

- **Equity** = owners or shareholders capital; i.e. the amount of money you started your business or occasionally put into the business, i.e. invested cash (capital);

- **Fixed Assets**, aka "non-current assets" = your plant and machinery + purchased business/commercial property + any asset that cannot be converted (i.e. non-liquid) into cash within a short period time------usually less than a year;

- **Gross Profit** = Sales – Cost of Sales;

- **% Mark-up** = selling price – cost of goods   x   100

cost of goods

This figure should be greater than 100%, preferably 300%;

- **Net Income** = gross profit, aka "operating profit" = your sales revenue (gross income) - cost of sales

A negative number here implies a loss situation!

- **Net Profit** = gross profit + other income – total expenses;

- **Net Profit after tax** = net profit – company tax payable;

- **Net worth,** aka "shareholders equity" = total assets – total liabilities.

% Profit margin (aka margin) before tax

$$= \frac{\text{net profit before tax}}{\text{sales}} \times 100$$

- **Sales,** aka "total income" or "turnover" = sales volume, e.g. quantity sold x sale price per unit sold;

- **Selling Price** = cost of goods x %Mark-up;

- **Total Equity** = capital + accumulated profits;

- **Total Costs** = fixed costs + all variable costs or expenses;

- **Total Liabilities,** aka "total debt" = current liabilities + long term loans;

- **Total Current Assets** = stock on hand + current assets;

- **Total Assets** = current assets + fixed assets

- **Return on Investment** = gross profit / owner's equity

This figure should be greater than 35%

To obtain a rough idea of the value of your business, calculate the average turnover (revenue) of the past 3 years and multiply this figure by 3.

There are many other more complex equations on the internet to estimate the selling or purchase price of an established business; each formula is specific to the type of business, e.g. retail, medical practitioners, architects, etc.

My equation that will give you a good idea of how your business is growing and what, in real terms, profit you are making, is:

(Net Profit as % of net turnover) - your price increase for that year – predicted economy growth for that year.

Example: (R10 800/R430 000) x 100 – 10% -2.7%

= 2.5% - 10% - 2.7%

i.e. your business had an actual loss and a negative growth rate for that year; you should have increased your prices by 12.5% to break even.

EXAMPLES of Financial Statements.

Income Statement (aka Profit and Loss Statement)

For the year ending 2013 of BeltsforU (Pty) Ltd

INCOME		Rand
Sales		560,000
Less: cost of sales		130,000
Gross Profit		430,000
Other income:		
Interest received		800
Total income		430,800
EXPENSES:		
Less:		420,000
Rent	125,000	
Electricity and water	4,000	
Insurance	3,000	
Salaries and wages	225,000	
Stationery and printing	1,000	
Advertising	9,000	
Telephone	1,000	
Repairs and maintenance	2,000	
Depreciation @ 20%pa	50,000	
Net profit before taxation		10,800
Less Company tax @ 28%		3,024
Profit after taxation		7,776

Balance Sheet

As at 28th February 2013 of BeltsforU (Pty) Ltd

CAPITAL EMPLOYED		Rand
Issued or share capital		100,000
Accumulated profit (loss)		15,200
Long term loans		195,000
		310,200

EMPLOYMENT OF CAPITAL:		
Fixed Assets		250,000
Current Assets:	54,000	
Inventory or stock	33,000	
Accounts receivable or debtors	5,000	
Bank and cash deposits	16,000	
Total Assets		304,000
Less: Current Liabilities:		243,800
Accounts payable or creditors	3,000	
Company taxation @ 28%	3,024	
Net current assets		60,200
		310,200

Banking

Your bank will send you a monthly statement either by post or email (eStatement). You must scrutinise this statement and compare it (reconcile) with what you have in your books of account. This check list, usually prepared regularly by your bookkeeper, is known as the Bank Reconciliation Statement. Basically it is a check to see that your bank has not deducted amounts unknown to you.

There is a difference between a bank "Debit Order" and a bank "Stop Order". The former is processed by your supplier instructing your bank to pay the supplier regularly (usually monthly); whereas the latter is processed by yourself instructing your bank to pay your supplier regularly (usually monthly).

You should never have your personal bank account at the same bank as your business account, for security and tax (SARS) reasons.

NOTES:

Suggest you list here your budget for YOUR business:

Chapter 9

Budget

What is a Budget

A budget is essentially a financial plan of how much money you expect to make over a certain period of time, against how much money you expect to spend in making this money. A budget could be considered similar to your Cash Flow Statement.

You must have a budget on paper; not keep one in your head. Many small business owners think that they can plan finances on a day to day basis......this is dangerous. Plan for the unexpected, as it will happen, it is not a question of "if" but "when". A budget must be part of your business plan.

You can use the many bookkeeping computer programmes available (see Chapter 8 above) to help you to compile a budget (your current budget should be based, somewhat, on previous financial statements). Budgets need to be updated regularly (at least every six months).

Preferably have two budgets: one calculated on the worst case scenario and the other based on the most optimistic scenario. Make sure that you budget for a profit not a deficit (loss)! If you operate between these two budgets, then you should be fairly safe from any financial crises.

You must compare your budget with your current financial records to see if you are operating within your budget. This is one of the sole purposes of having a budget!

"Beware of little expenses. A small leak will sink a great ship"

----------quote from Benjamin Franklin

NOTES:

Suggest you list here a basic budget of proposed income against estimated expenses for YOUR business:

Chapter 10

Cash Flow

What is Cash Flow? **This is the most important aspect of any business.**

Cash flow is essentially the movement of cash (your cash receipts or "accounts receivable") from your customers/debtors to your bank account (i.e. receiving income) to paying out cash to your suppliers/creditors ("accounts payable")......**it is just a matter of the correct timing of these two events,** to avoid bankruptcy!

Here the word "cash" literally means cash or something that can within days or weeks (not months, years) be converted into cash (i.e. cash in the bank).

You must make sure that you have at least **3 months cash** reserves or savings accounts such as money market savings, to cover your monthly fixed and variable expenses; as a financial contingency plan.

Many businesses have gone out of business due to insufficient "own funds" to cover these expenses in times of below average turnover. Do not borrow extra funds from a bank or go deeper into your overdraft facility; rather decrease your variable expenses, such as holding stock and/or consumables such as stationery.

If you have stock on the shelves that are collecting dust, SELL IT at cost price! Stock not turning over into cash is costing you storage/shelf space!

You may also ask staff to take their annual leave due at this time. If no paid leave is due, then as a last resort, request diplomatically for them to take unpaid leave. Note that non-loyal staff would probably seek alternative employment when your business is financially unstable. However, you as the owner must persevere at times like this to keep going. If you are committed to your business, as you should be, then you will pull through. Reward your staff that are loyal.

*If you are not a cash only business, then you must send out your invoices or debit notes to your customers/clients as soon as possible (the sooner your invoices/debit notes go out, the sooner you will receive your money)..........this is just common logic. Also you should only pay your creditors/suppliers on the last day of the following month so that you can receive bank interest on your savings; for example, utilise or gear the money you receive from your customer before you have paid your supplier.

Unfortunately this is why large corporations follow the same procedure and take 90 days or more to pay their suppliers (i.e. you) and hence they become richer at your expense!

Also remember that, in reality, you have to pay output VAT periodically to SARS on the invoices (sales) that you have sent out to your customers before you get paid by your customers (who are claiming their input VAT. Remember you just collect vat taxes for SARS, free of charge to the taxman!).

If you carry stock, just consider that stock is your money "tied up" on the shelf, so the longer you take to sell your stock the worse your cash flow situation will be.

Credit control in a small business is critical for survival. Credit control is essentially the collection of cash on time, which is due to you. Check out Example 8 at back of book.

However, don't throw good money after bad money. What this means is that it costs money to track down and attempt to recover outstanding monies owed to you...............these costs (initially about 30% of the bad debt amount) could escalate into a loss situation for the sale or service that you had provided to this defaulting customer or client.

Always follow the legal procedure in trying to collect outstanding monies. The safest procedure is to hand them over to a registered debt collector, or your attorney, after a written warning by you to the defaulting customer.

Litigation with attorneys is very expensive..........the only people who make money here, are the attorneys on both sides (i.e. your attorney and the defaulting customer's attorney)! As a rough guide, any monies less than R10,000.00 owing to you, is not worth the services of an attorney. A cheaper way is to retain the services of an arbitrator, but check his/her fees first. Otherwise, ask your accountant to write it off as a non-recoverable bad debt and claim the amount as a taxable deduction.

Beware, if you ever need to retain the services of an attorney, or a consultant, his or her fees and future litigation costs might not be an allowable tax deduction (by the tax man) from your normal course of business operations.

A word of caution, if you ever require the services of an attorney, always check yourself that he or she is currently registered with the statutory law society. Also retain the services of one that is willing to fight for your rights irrespective of what the law books state. The "law" is not just. Government Acts, corporate law, common law and case law are all a matter of personal interpretation by practising lawyers! That is why there are so many lawyers in life. Check also if there is any possibility of a conflict of interest between your attorney and the other party's attorney.

Prescription is when a debt (for example, obligation to pay money) is extinguished after a period of time. Usually, in general day to day business dealings this is 3 years from the date of issue of demand (e.g. invoice or debt note) from you to your customer. This means that if you don't collect this customer defaulting on his or her debt, then on or after 3years the debt has lapsed or prescribed. Check out the latest amendments to this very important piece of legislature (Prescription Act 68 of 1969) that protects the *bad* paying customer.

"Creditors have better memories than debtors"
"Remember that creditor is money"
----------*quotes from Benjamin Franklin*

NOTES:

Suggest you list here your cash and capital requirements for YOUR business:

Chapter 11

Pricing or Costing

What is pricing (costing)?
This is the price that you are going to charge your customers/clients for your goods or services that you are going to or are providing to the marketplace (your customers).

This is another very critical aspect of your business and it is essential that you get it *"right"*; however there is no such thing as the "right" price or tariff of fees. You will have to adjust this price from time to time as the market changes. Remember that your target market is forever changing, unless you are in a trade such as plumbing.

Here are some ways of determining what price you should be charging (cost analysis):

1. check out what your competition is charging;

2. calculate what it costs you to buy raw materials, manufacture, process, etc. your product, then add on at least 130% to this "cost of sale" price; if you charge less than the 130%, then you might as well put your money (capital) into a bank savings account earning 10% interest compounded;

3. note that these mark-up prices (see 2 above) can run from 130% to over 300% depending on what the market will take; it is a matter of general economics of the "supply and demand".

4. also, consider customer discounts, loyalty vouchers, rebates, etc., when marketing your price to your customers/clients;

5. always use the psychological pricing format, that is, if you calculate that you want to sell your goods at R56.00, then advertise your price at R55.99; as this latter price appears cheaper to your customer than the former price.

The closest to the *correct* or *right* price, is the price that a customer/client is prepared to pay for your goods or services.

VAT----a much misunderstood but critical aspect of your business.

Vat (Value Added Tax) or Sales Tax, is basically the government's share of your sale price. You have to collect the Vat from your customers (even before your customers pay you) on behalf of the government. Check with your bookkeeper or accountant with respect to the current rates and type of Vat that have to be charged to your customers/clients.

There are essentially two parts, namely "input vat" and "output vat". The difference is what you pay over to the government (SARS---also known as the Receiver of Revenue or the taxman). The "input vat" is that portion of the cost that your supplier of goods or services charges you. The "output vat" is that portion of the vat that you have to add onto your selling price and charge your customers; thus it is supposed to be the tax on the *value* that you have added (e.g. by manufacturing raw materials into a final product) to your product before selling it.

Note that, in most instances, you are required to register as a Vat Vendor, but check with your accountant.

If you are registered, you are required to submit to SARS, regular Vat Returns; this is where you can claim the "input vat" which is then deducted from your "output vat" and the balance must then be paid over to the taxman before a certain date.

Also refer to Chapter 8 above.

Paying your vat portion over to SARS when you have insufficient cash funds, have caused many small businesses to financially collapse! **You could become insolvent just because of your Vat liabilities!**

"Let no feeling of discouragement prey upon you, and in the end you are sure to succeed."
----------quote from Abraham Lincoln

NOTES:

Suggest you list here some estimated selling prices for YOUR business and then research them or use them for short periods of time to see which might be your correct selling price to the public:

Chapter 12

Resources

What are Resources?
These are the "tools" that you require in order to operate your business.

Examples are:

- "plant & machinery" (aka FIXED ASSETS) that is equipment that is necessary to make your goods;

- "staff/employees" or even yourself (aka HUMAN RESOURCES), that is the people needed to operate the "plant & machinery" and to finally sell or distribute your finished goods or services;

- "service providers" (or outsourced resources), these are the persons or companies that provide essential services to your business; e.g. water and electricity supplier, website and email hosting, accountant, financial service providers, etc.;

- "stock" the amount of raw materials to make your goods, or the amount of finished goods stored;

- "cash" the amount of ready cash on hand or in the bank.

Fixed Assets (Assets Register)

It is a legal requirement to keep a record of all capital "plant & machinery" items, immovable assets and other high value assets, other than cash. This record is known as an "ASSETS REGISTER". This register could be extracted from your bookkeeping data. The Assets Register is also useful for insurance purposes to assist you to estimate what insurance coverage you need, as well as estimating losses when there is a claim. Refer to Insurance, Chapter 16. The word *capital* is used where that "plant & machinery" was purchased for a large value (e.g. in excess R10,000.00 for small businesses). An Assets Register is also a requirement under the Companies Act. Your insurance company may also insist that you keep and update such a register.

Finance (Capital)

There are many financial service providers or banks in South Africa that will lend you "start-up capital" for new businesses, or "working capital" for improvements, new stock, etc. Check out the Yellow Pages or the internet for organisations that lend money. But **be aware of hidden costs** that they charge over and above their interest rates, such as monthly administration fees, ledger or ancillary bank fees, and "*due diligence*" fees. The "*due diligence*" fees could cost thousands of rand; this is the so-called costs to the financial service provider for checking your credit worthiness and risk ratings.

Staff (Human Resources)

One of the most important assets of any business is its staff/employees. Employees can make or break a business irrespective of the size of the business. Hence, try to hire only the best available, but beware, most of the best of the younger generation usually jump from employer to employer depending who offers them the higher salary or remuneration package; hence incorporate fringe benefits such as performance bonuses, travelling allowances, company smart phones, computer tablets, etc.; to encourage them to stay in your employment. As a general rule, an employee should bring into the business (financial worth, productivity) at least 3x (three times) their salary package. Generally, new employees only become productive in their third month or fourth month of employment.

To train new staff, costs money and a lot of wasted unproductive time. Remember that wasted "TIME" in any business, costs (*lost or opportunity costs*) money.

The objective for any business is to have the minimum number of employees to achieve maximum profitability, in the long term.

When promoting staff take into consideration *Peter's Principle*, which states that a competent employee in a specific job position, would be promoted successfully to the next higher levels; until **that** next level is his/hers level of incompetence of that highest job position. An example is where a very productive sales person is promoted to sales manager but has no management capabilities and hence becomes a very ineffective sales manager. Promotion is not the only answer to rewarding above average productive staff; other ways are extra annual leave, shorter working hours, flexitime, travel concessions, smartphone reimbursements, etc.

There are many HR policies that you should have in operation. Some of these are listed below:

- Organogram or Organisational Chart, showing how each staff member of your business fits into the business structure; basically it shows who reports to whom and who is responsible for what department or function of the business;

- Job Description, there must be a written job description for each and every job position (and employee) in your business. This should describe the duties and responsibilities of the incumbent/employee. Generally, the "Letter of Appointment" may be sufficient to cover these areas and to dictate working conditions. It is advisable to supply each employee with both these documents, and get them to sign an acknowledgement of understanding and of receipt thereof;

- Job Grading. The *Paterson Grading System* is well known in South Africa. It is basically a grading philosophy, based on levels (generally 10 levels) of decision making, different levels of competence, length of service and the responsibility of the various types of job positions in a company. A salary range is then assigned to each grade. Example:

Grade	Position	*Salary units*	Salary range, annual (approx.)
A	General labourer/cleaner/unskilled	1x	R36,000- R48,000
B1	Semi-Skilled worker/factory operator	1.3x	R46,800-R56,000
B2	Semi-Skilled worker but auto routine jobs	1.6x	R57,600-R80,000
C1	Skilled, Qualified worker/student engineer	3x	R108,000-R150,000
C2	Skilled routine work Supervisor/superintendent	5x	R180,000-R200,000
D1	Line or middle management	6x	R216,000-R350,000
D2	Middle management/Factory Manager	10x	R360,000-R1,000,000
E	Senior or General management/Branch Manager	50x	>R1,800,000
F1	Executive management and policy makers	100x	>R3,600,000
F2	Directors/CEO	200x	>R7,200,000

There are other staff evaluation systems such as, Hay Grading or Appraisal, JE Manager and Peromnes.

Use the minimum salary of R36,000 pa as a *"salary base unit"*, then it becomes easy to establish what an employee should be earning by using the Table above.

A reasonable annual salary increase for a worker is about 10%.

- Time Books, Clock Cards or computerized access controls (preferably biometric systems) must be in place. You must know what days your staff work and their hours of productive work; this documentation must be kept up to date to avoid many problems with staff and labour inspectors;

- "Restraint of Trade" contracts, here seek the advice of your lawyer;

- "Disciplinary Code" is where there must be a written disciplinary policy so that employees know what are the business rules of behaviour and the consequences or penalties of breaking these company rules. These rules often cover theft, insubordination, sexual harassment, and many other minor misdemeanours;

- Also, there has to be a written "Grievance Procedure" where an employee has the opportunity to make reasonable accusations against a fellow employee (irrespective of whether the fellow employee is a senior or subordinate), where he or she is of the opinion, that they have been mistreated, discriminated against or instructed to do a job not within their job description;

- Written policies of applicable Standard Operating Procedures (SOP) to your type of business.

- For new staff you must issue them with a "Letter of Appointment" stating their starting wage or salary, the starting date of the employment, their working days and hours. This document should also refer to the applicable "Job Description" of the position (refer to above).

- "Employment Contract". This standard document (as prescribed by the Basic Conditions of Employment Act) must be completed and issued to all employees. This document should also cover, in more detail, the working conditions, any probationary periods, confidentially of your business operations, procedure for set-off of any debts incurred by the employee to you; also include your company's HR policies. It supplements the "Letter of Appointment" and "Job Description".

Examples of some of these documents are at back of this book. Also check out an interviewer's guide to questions that you should ask of job applicants; refer to Example 11.

Your management and peoples skills are critical when dealing with staff. Be consistent with rewarding or disciplining.........do not have favourites. Below is an excellent piece of advice that you can give your staff; it was written many decades ago by an unknown executive of a major Chinese bank, to his employees:

1. *Don't lie. It wastes my time and yours and I am sure to catch you in the end.*

2. *Watch your work and not the clock. A long day's work makes a short day long, a short day's work makes my face long.*

3. *Give me more than I expect and I will pay you more than you expect. I can afford to increase your pay if you increase my profits.*

4. *Don't do anything that hurts self-respect. The employee who is capable of stealing for me is capable of stealing from me.*

5. *Don't tell me what I want to hear, but what I ought to hear. I don't want a valet for my vanity, but for my money.*

6. *Dishonesty is never an accident.*

7. *It's none of my business what you do at night, but if dissipation affects what you do the next day, you will last half as long in my employment as you had hoped.*

8. *Don't kick if I kick. If you are worth correcting, you're worth keeping.*

Another piece of useful advice for your staff, from an unknown author:

A successful business man was once asked the secret of his success. "I'll tell you," he replied. "It was a game I played. I pretended I owned the place...lock, stock and barrel."

Isn't it strange? At home, we worry if we leave one unnecessary light on all night, or if someone we've hired to repair our stove does a sloppy job. But in the office or at the plant, we'll waste electricity, equipment, materials, time and workmanship and never bat an eye.

Why? Because we think of the business as "it", and profit or loss as "theirs". On the other hand, at home, we think of it as wasting "my" money and its "my" loss.

Really, they are one and the same. Loss by the company must be absorbed by the profit, and each one of us shares in the profit. So we too can play a game with ourselves. It goes something like this: "When I waste at the plant or the office....I am wasting "my" time, "my" job security and "my" future.

Stop and consider how often each day we throw away cents on the job. In the office, each time a good paper clip is bent out of shape, or usable copy paper is thrown into a waste basket............cents are lost. Waste occurs through carelessness and neglect.

Carelessness which resulted in but ten cents of material or service being wasted often times, seems insignificant to the employee involved. Suppose each of our employees work 245 days a year. At an average of ten cents a day, he or she would have thrown away R24.50 a year. Multiply this figure by the number of employees in the business, say 30, we get R735.00 a year. This amount could be staggering for a small business.

It is the cumulative cost of fractional waste that adds up to big money. Each employee has a personal stake in keeping costs down. Remember, every cent you save means that much more opportunity for you.

Delegate tasks to staff which you know that they can handle. A major disrupting factor in any business is staff that are untrained and/or inexperienced for certain tasks.

You must outsource tasks that you or your staff are not competent to undertake. But first do your sums! Can you afford to outsource or should you not venture into that sale or production run?

Keep your staff busy (give them slightly more work than they can handle in a day); *an idle mind is the workshop of the devil!*

Other Resources (the Market Place)

Yes, your market or customer base can be considered a *resource*!

You must stay in contact with your customers, after all, it is repeat business from the same customers that can make or break a business. It costs you more money (said to be 5 times) to attract new customers than it costs to keep regular customers!

Know what your customer/market wants today and what they want tomorrow; plan accordingly your advertising, building or office expansion plans, future staff complements, etc., refer to Chapter 15.

Here are some useful websites:

- http://southafrica.smetoolkit.org
- http://www.sba.gov/smallbusinessplanner/index.html
- http://www.seda.co.za
- http://www.sabusinesshub.co.za
- http://www.businessdictionary.com
- http://www.helpbizowners.com
- For up to date financial news go to the Financial Mail interactive site at: http://www.fm.co.za.
- The SA Law Society is at: http://www.lssa.org.za
- http://www.agreementsonline.co.za

For capital or funds try these organisations:

- Industrial Development Corporation at: http://www.idc.co.za

- Rand Merchant Bank's Corvest division at: http://www.rmbcorvest.co.za.

- For assistance and financial help, try Business Partners at: http://www.businesspartners.co.za

- Also many of the large banks have a small business development division. Check with your banker or accountant.

In summary:

- The most critical resources are staff and equipment.

- It is no good having the latest equipment or machinery if your staff are incompetent or untrained.

- On the other hand, it is no good having competent staff if your equipment or machinery is always faulty or out of service.

- Do not have idle equipment/machinery........it is lost opportunity income. If possible, incorporate another work shift so that your machinery is utilised 24 hours a day.

- Do not have idle staff........they are a waste of your precious money.

- Do not borrow money on borrowed money; gearing of financials is not an amateur's game.

NOTES:

Suggest you make a list here of the required resources for YOUR business:

Chapter 13

Advertising and Public Relations

What is advertising?

Advertising is basically a form of conveying to your market (your customers or clients) of what your business is all about and what you can offer that your competitors cannot offer.

You must entice existing and potential customers to buy your products/services!

All your business stationery, such as letterheads, catalogues, price lists, compliment slips, fax and email headers, brochures, websites, etc., must have same formats, type fonts and colours. This is critical so that the public can sub-consciously recognize (remember) a document being from your organization. You should restrict your business colours to maximum of three; also make sure that these colours are compatible (use the colour-wheel). If in doubt, seek advice from a professional printer (person not the machine) or other suitable creative art design person. Or you might want to seek the advice of a *"Feng Shui"* expert, if you have faith in that philosophy.

The text in advertisements or brochures should be clear, legible and not be subject to misinterpretation; it must have credibility (i.e. it must be ethical and show integrity).

Effective advertising is repetitive advertising.

Your company logo is as critical as your business name. It should represent or symbolize what your business is all about. Every curve, line, arch or polygon including colours, exists for a reason; and that is to identify your company or brand. Do not have more than 3 colours (of which one may be red, as red is considered lucky) which must be compatible (easy on the eye as well as "website/browser friendly").

Your website and its domain name are very crucial to your business survival; it is the technological progression from the telephone printed yellow pages to online advertising. You can build your website (there are many so-called free website programmes on the internet), or preferably get an expert to do it for you. See below for more information.

Social Media/Newsletters

Newsletters, blogs, *tweets* and internet social media are types of advertising, but DO NOT use these for blatant self-promotion of your business. Customers or clients would like to read in the newsletters items of NEWS about:

- your business;
- changes in staff so that they know whom they are dealing with;
- general news about the industry or profession that you operate in;
- any useful reference material that they may refer to in the future.

The main object here is that once your customer/client has read the newsletter or blog, irrespective of whether it is in email format or hard copy, you would want them to store it for future reference. Newsletters, as well as emails, must be a means of communication between your business and your market.

A hardcopy newsletter (although out-of-date now) should not be more than a page long; both sides of page may be printed. Make sure that you have listed your latest contact details.

Always keep in contact with your customers/clients.

The latest (in place of the customary hardcopy newsletters) is to participate in social media networks such as *Facebook*, *Twitter*, *LinkedIn* and various internet blogs. You can also paste a newsletter page on your website. *Google* offers a free blogging site and service.

You must market your business with integrity and authenticity about your products or service that you sell to your customers or clients. No buyer likes to be "*ripped off*" or "*scammed*" by a business, whether small or a major corporation.

Your relationship with your customers/clients must be based on a type of unofficial "partnership in business" contract.

Referrals from your customers are the best and cheapest way of advertising.

Customers buy from people that they like. This statement is important. Business is essentially communication between one set of people (you and your staff) and the other set of people (your customers or clients) and their staff.

Websites and Domains

You **must have** a website even if you are only a small local business. Your viewers (visitors) of your website will be directed firstly to local websites, because the latest web browsers (Internet Explorer, Google's Chrome, Microsoft Bing, Apple Safari and Mozilla's Firefox) will automatically link to those websites of where your computer is situated.

Yes! Microsoft, Google and others do track, at least, what country you are located, even city; from your computer's IP address. Every computer or device on the internet has its own IP address.

Domain names are used to identify an IP address on the internet. For example, the domain name *beltsforus.com* represents an IP address that consists of a row of four numbers each having three digits, such as 064.004.011.042. Domain names are used to identify particular web pages. For example, in the URL *http://www.beltsforus.com/index.html,* the domain name is *beltsforus.com.*

You can build your own website. It is quite easy, you just need to know the simple basics of HTML 5 and CSS 3 coding.......many books and free internet lessons on these small computer scripts, are available. Make sure you chose your business colours correctly; here it is useful to use a "Colour Wheel" to select compatible colours. Suggest not more than 3 colours (Triad principle). For customer interactivity on your website you will need some of the popular JavaScript coding.

There are many free website design programmes on the internet (such as www.CoffeeCup.com, www.BlueVoda.com, and www.joomla.org), but these have somewhat limited flexibility (i.e. if you want to change something) and interactivity, but always have built in "cookies".

Alternatively, you could hire a professional web design company; but they are expensive.........BEWARE that they do not copyright (ownership) of your website into their name! Check who are the owners (registrant) of your website on http://tools.whois.net. The most popular international website character set is UTF-8; so make sure that your website is written in this character coding and not ASCII.

Your website should contain the following webpages:

- A *Home Page* (generally a file named as index.html, this is similar to a front door, entrance or reception area to your business;

- *About Us* page, informs visitor a bit more about what your business is all about and how it came to be in existence;

- *Contact Us*, generally lists staff or department contact details;

- *Privacy Policy*, it is a link that is generally at the bottom of each webpage or footer, describing your policy with respect to the information that you gather online about your visitors;

- Landing pages, these are your products or services pages, i.e. these are the most important pages....they sell your products or services.

Intellectual property

You must create a brand or trademarks and protect your business names, logos, formulations and recipes, packaging designs, copyrights, domain names and slogans. You can get your friends, family and customers to help you to create a logo and slogan; otherwise to obtain the services of a marketing agent and creative artist will be very costly. Whichever of these items are applicable to your type of business, you must have them patented and registered.

In South Africa you need to do this with the Companies and Intellectual Properties Commission Office (CIPC); your business bank manager, accountant or attorney can assist you here.

These trademarks or branding assist the public in identifying you from your competition. Not only are they a great advantage in marketing and sales, but they also increase the value of your business especially when or if you decide to sell. You can ask your accountant to list this value in your Balance Sheet.

There are various types or classes of trademarks such as traditional or ordinary and the certification marks such as the SABS mark.

You can register by lodging form TM1 with www.cipc.co.za, a trade mark for your business name, logo, slogan and even your domain name (website).

Customer Care

What is Public Relations?

Public Relations are now your "customer care" policies and procedures when dealing with customer queries and complaints.

Also how does your receptionist or telephone operator treat customers/clients when they make contact with your business? Are they polite or rude? Check it out and you will be surprised how your staff is handling your customers or potential customers!

If you sell or provide a service to a customer/client and he/she is not too happy about the sale/deal, then you can be sure that he/she is not going to come back, but also he/she might bad-mouth your organisation. **One unsatisfied customer** will tell **five people** about their bad experiences with your business. It has been proved that customers remember us for our shoddy service, but quickly forget about our competence or excellent customer care. This is because everybody expects competent and excellent service as well as after sales service.......you have been warned! It has been said that it costs 15 times more expensive to get back a customer that you have lost, then to attract a new customer.

It is a lot less expensive to retain regular customers. It is the satisfied and regular customers that bring in the money........SHOW ME THE MONEY! This is what business is all about.

Remember that it does not matter what type of business you have, the bottom line is that you are SELLING yourself, your staff and your business image to the outside world!

Imbed into the minds of your employees that it is the *customer*, not you, that pays for their salaries, bonuses and other benefits.

Identify your loyal customers and those few who bring in more than 80% of your turnover. Treat them with extra discounts and favours Serve them with utmost respect and always "go the extra mile" for them, as they are literally the support of your business.

"The only place where success comes before work is in the dictionary"

----------*quote from Vidal Sassoon*

NOTES:

Suggest you list here how you are going to sell YOUR products:

Chapter 14

Market Research

What is Market Research?

Market research is basically where you determine what you have to offer for sale and whether there actually is a market (customers/clients) out there that are willing and able to buy what you are selling, whether it is goods (customers) or a service (clients). Market research is something that you should have done before starting or purchasing your own small business.

Market research does not stop once you have got your business going profitably.

An ongoing market research is getting to know what your competitors are doing, but not letting them know what you are doing or planning to do.

Remember when you are networking with your peers or competitors at various seminars, trade shows, etc., listen to what is being said and study what is being done, but keep your mouth closed about your own business plans.

However, if you are networking with potential customers/clients, then inform them of how you (i.e. your business) can add value to their products or their business......DO NOT brag or overdo your personal capabilities or those of your business. People do not like *braggers*. Your potential customers/clients need to know what's in it for them. They need **value** for their money that they are going to spend on you!

You can do your market research by:

- posting out flyers (pamphlets, circulars, email marketing);

- placing a survey questionnaire on the internet;

- hiring temporary staff to canvass people (potential customers) at shopping malls;

- social networking;

- also, hiring an outside agency to do the market research for you (this is very expensive).

Once you have all this data and information, you must process or analyse it. Here you will need to separate the data into demographic sectors applicable to your type of business and then draw conclusions, and finally make plans.

"Success is walking from failure to failure with no loss of enthusiasm"

----------quote from Winston Churchill

NOTES:

Suggest you list here YOUR market findings, including who your competitors are; for your type of business:

Chapter 15

Strategic Planning

W hat is Strategic Planning?

It is basically how and what you want to do in the future. This can also be a follow-up to your market research. Here you must plan at least 5 years ahead for a small business; 10 to 15 years ahead for larger businesses. In other words, what or where do you want your business to be in 5 years' time? What will you be selling or manufacturing in that future time?

This is where you must get all your senior staff members, partners, directors, etc. together and have a "Think Tank" meeting where everyone *throws around* ideas. Then, these ideas are (*thrown into a tank*) somewhat put together (*mixed and stirred*) until you come up with some feasible plans (*product*). This is known also as *brainstorming*. This is also the approach that you should have taken to research your dreams and ideas before starting your own business.

One must remember that the economy and your market WILL change over a period of time. You must be able to foresee from your particular type of business and experience, what this time period is and what will change.

Even your area of location of your business might no longer be suitable in 5 years' time.

Any type of business or organisation must have some sort of aim to which present and future decisions must be taken with this goal in mind.

So, get busy now and plan for the future before it catches you unaware which could devastate, or worse bankrupt your business.

Your business must do things (or offer after-sales services) that your competitors fail to do. Go the "extra mile" for your customers/clients. Why should new customers come to you instead of going to your competition? Pretend that you are a customer, and ask yourself the question as to why **you** should go to that business (your business) for those goods/services?

Your ongoing market research should be taken into consideration when doing your strategic planning.

There are many online survey programmes; a free one is at www.surveymonkey.com.

You must not work **in** your business, but work **on** your business! What this means is that you must not do the daily tasks as an employee (you hire someone else to do this), but you must do the planning, organising, implementing, quotations and tenders. Also, checking that all your workers are doing what they are hired to do and doing it correctly in the stipulated time frame; this requires constant vigilance on your part.

You must be flexible and be ready to change with the times.

One of the biggest risks to small business today, is cybercrime. Don't think that just because you are a small business that computer hackers or ransomware are not going to infiltrate your IT structure (computers, servers, databases, websites, cloud and emails; even your social media communications or links. Hackers will go for the easiest targets where businesses cannot afford to have or install 3rd layer firewalls, or even retain IT specialists. You must plan and protect for these events.

NOTES:

What is your strategic plan or ultimate goal for YOUR business?

What do you do that your competition does not provide?

Chapter 16

Insurance

What is insurance?

Insurance is a form of guarantee that if or when a prescribed event takes place, or a prescribed time period has elapsed, then a certain amount of money or other compensation shall be paid by another person/company (known as the insurer) to you (known as the insured); in exchange for a monthly or annual premium/fee.

The concept here, is to place the insured (you or your business) back into the same position that you were **before** the loss or damage occurred, not a better position.

Inflating an insurance claim is fraud; rather get an independent estimate/quote before claiming on your policy.

Note that insurance is NOT an investment and there is no return on the monies spent by yourself or your business.

If you are insured for the same event by two insurance companies (i.e. you have two policies), you will not be paid out twice. The insurance companies will haggle amongst themselves as to who will pay you out or at what *pro rata* will each pay. Thus, make sure you are not double insured paying two lots of unnecessary premiums.........this can sometimes happen with vehicle insurance and "All Risks" policies.

In the case of an insured vehicle, make sure that you have informed your insurance company of the names of the regular drivers, as this might be pertinent in the event of a successful claim.

An insurance company will only pay out, on a vehicle policy, the current market or retail value of the vehicle in the event of a total loss; irrespective of whether the vehicle was insured for a greater amount.

Hence, you should regularly check the current value of your vehicles and get your broker/agent to adjust the premiums accordingly........you might be giving your money away to the insurance companies on paying unnecessary high premiums!

An insurance **broker** is supposedly an independent person/company who endeavours to obtain the widest insurance cover for you, from all the insurance companies, at the lowest cost to you.

An insurance **agent** is a person/company who acts on behalf of a particular insurance company or selected companies.

Both charge commission/fees; in some cases these can be negotiated.

Always check and make sure that you are dealing with a broker and not an agent. In the event of a claim, a broker is supposed to act on your behalf (the insured) and that of the insurer to obtain a mutually satisfactory settlement, whereas most agents will have only the interests of their principals (the insurance company).

Beware of other hidden fees or charges. Many brokers/agents will inform you that you don't pay their commission fees. This is not entirely true as the insurance company will pay their commissions, but indirectly you are charged for this in your premiums.

Alternatively, you can go direct to the insurance companies asking for quotes and comparing these. Thus, here you can save, maybe up to 15% off your premium.

It is a myth that insurance is only for those wealthy businesses, but it is the business owner who cannot afford the cost of unforeseen breakdown repairs or replacement of machinery, that needs insurance.

Security of your business and premises is critical when it comes to insurance. Your premiums could increase drastically if you have many claims due to burglaries and similar events, over a short period of time. The higher the risk (as ascertained by the insurance company and their actuary), the higher your premium.

In determining your risk profile, ultimately your premium, the insurance companies take into consideration the following:

- type of business or occupation;
- location of your premises;
- condition of the buildings;
- level of any on site security;
- type and condition of alarm systems and service provider, if any;
- type risks that you insured;
- your claims history, usually taken over the past 5 years.

The **most important clause** in any short-term policy is that of the "AVERAGE CLAUSE", as this has the effect of a reduced claim pay-out. It works somewhat like this:

> Say your machinery has been valued by a "Loss Adjuster" or certified valuator, at R100,000. However, unwittingly, you insured it for only R60,000. In the event of a claim the insurer will only pay out on the R60,000 policy. You put in a claim for R80,000. Hence the insurance will only pay out R48,000 (less the "excess" or sometimes referred to as "First amount payable", see below). You are considered to be your own insurer for the balance of the R40,000.
>
> Thus, the insurance company calculation is

$$\text{Average Clause} = \frac{\text{sum insured} \times \text{loss claimed}}{\text{total value}}$$

$$\text{Average Clause} = \frac{60{,}000 \times 80{,}000}{100{,}000} = 48{,}000$$

The "Loss Adjuster/Assessor" is a qualified person who assesses the size or value of an insurance claim on behalf of the insurance company. He/she may or may not be employed by the insurer (insurance company).

Another clause is the **"First Amount Payable or Excess"**. This is the amount *payable* by you, i.e. that part of a loss for which you are liable, in the event of a successful claim; basically if this amount was R5,000 (or that amount as stated in your policy), then in the above example the insurer would only pay you out R48,000 – R5,000 = R43,000!.

WHAT YOU ONLY GOT BACK R43,000 ON A CLAIM OF R80,000!!!!

Thus, you were considered to be "under insured"

The "First Amount Payable" is negotiable with the insurer, usually if you volunteer to accept a higher amount then the compulsory amount (excess), then your premiums are reduced; but make sure that you can sustain this excess figure in the event of a claim.

Also pay special attention to the clause **"Special Exclusions"** in your policy. This is where the insurer has not covered you for certain events occurring.

Other important terms are:

- "consequential loss" is a loss directly arising from another loss, e.g. loss of profits or business interruption clause, after a fire;

- "escalation clause", in a policy is when the sum insured increases through the period of insurance in step with the assumed rate of inflation; e.g. an annual premium is cheaper than a monthly premium, but make sure you have, say, a 12% escalation clause, thus the monthly insured value increases by 1% per month to keep in step with your "Average Clause";

- *"Uberrima Fides"* means in good faith, i.e. all the information given by you to the insurer when applying or renewing a policy is assumed to be total and true. The insurer may refuse to pay out on a claim if it is discovered that you gave false or withheld pertinent information in your application, or during the course of the insurance policy. Note that if any insurable circumstances change during the insurance period, you are obliged to inform your insurance company;

- *"Force majeure"* means coverage for financial losses arising out of the inability of the insured to prevent an event such as earthquake, war, revolution, epidemics, etc. An "Act of God" is sometimes included in this clause.

- "Lapse" is when the termination of an insurance contract takes place due to non-payment of premiums, or by the insurer's decision not to renew a policy/contract.

Also beware of hidden **"Claims Preparation Costs"** charged by the insurer in the event of a claim.

There are different classes of **risk** which you must insure your business or yourself against. These could be the following (depending upon what type of small business you have):

- Assets All Risks (e.g. trade equipment kept in your car; laptops or smartphones that you keep with you or on you) and/or Goods in Transit;

- Burglary and similar crimes; plus any consequential damage to persons or property;

- Accidental damage (e.g. by employees) to critical equipment;

- Plate Glass (your shop window, this should be covered by your landlord, if you are a tenant);

- Office equipment (e.g. computers, ADSL modems, printers, electronic alarm systems) insure against power surcharges;

- Loss on Earnings or Business Interruption (e.g. machinery breakdowns, power outages, employee strikes, arson);

- Accounts Receivable (e.g. destruction of bookkeeping records of customers' accounts, in a fire);

- Water or flood damage (e.g. to stock, goods for sale, assets);

- Vehicle or fleet insurance, "comprehensive" or "balance third party, fire and theft";

- Delivery motor cycles and vans;

- Contractors All Risks (you must insist on any contractors working on your premises that they have their own insurance cover for their workmen; (here you need to request from the contractor their "Letter of Good Standing" from the government Compensation Fund Office);

- Currency fluctuations (if you are in export/import business, or even if you have any foreign customers or suppliers);

- Fidelity Guarantee (e.g. if your staff deal with cash, employee dishonesty and fraud);

- Fire Insurance (e.g. stock losses, etc.);

- Building insurance if you are the owner of your business premises;

- Pollution or Environmental Impairment/Indemnity (e.g. your accidental effluent discharges, etc.);

- Contractual Liability (e.g. you are unable to fulfil an order/contract due to unforeseen circumstances);

- Public Liability (e.g. injuries to customers whilst on your premises);

- Professional Indemnity (if you are sued for professional incompetence);

- Directors and Officers (D&O) policy;

- Trustees indemnity policy;

- Partnership Insurance (you should insure yourself and your partners for life or incapacity events);

- Group Personal Accident (a top-up on the Government "IOD" compulsory insurance);

- Cyber security and internet risks from ransomware, viruses, malware, internet "cloud" risks or your off-site servers;

- "Acts of God" which should be covered in all comprehensive policies, are events which take place due to natural causes such as storms, flooding, lightning and wildfires; causing loss of stock in trade, damage to furniture and fittings, etc.

Always check your policy once it has been issued to you, to make sure that you are covered by all possible contingencies pertaining to your type of business or trade. Also, the **correct name of the insured** person, company name or partnership, is on the policy, as this is important to avoid claims being dismissed on technicalities.

Always insure for the **replacement value** of your fixed and current assets. Replacement value is the cost to you to totally replace an asset; whereas market value is the depreciated value (similar to resale value) of an asset.

As mentioned elsewhere in this, your guidebook, your business circumstances will change from time to time and, hence, so will your insurance requirements. Therefore you must re-evaluate, with your broker or agent, your insurance needs at least every 2 years, preferably annually.

"If you don't' have a competitive advantage, don't compete"

----------*quote from Jack Welch*

NOTES:

Suggest you sketch a rough business plan, or your future plans here for YOUR business:

Chapter 17

Documentation and Records

All businesses have documents and records. The legal construction/terminology of contractual documents is critical. You must get the paperwork right on every aspect of your business.

There are many generic drafts on the internet, such as at www.agreementsonline.co.za, or "Google" it! Also you can obtain copies from your local Chamber of Commerce, or from some stationery shops.

Human Resource (personnel department) documents such as:

- time sheets or electronic clock-in cards,
- job or work cards/logs,
- staff leave application forms,
- termination of service certificates,
- letters of employment and/or contract of service agreements,
- disciplinary codes, staff grievance procedures,

These have to be available or in operation in any business enterprise. This is essential if you want to avoid staff problems in the future, also some of these employee documents are mandatory as they might be inspected by Government Labour Inspectors.

You also have to have other documents such as:

- credit or cash handling policies;
- mission and vision statements;
- mandatory staff notices;
- occupational health and safety inspections or audits (e.g. OHSA, SHEQ);
- Quality Management Systems (QMS) and Quality Policy;
- machine calibration or inspection certificates;
- business licenses;
- accreditation certification, where applicable;
- anti-bribery policies.

Check out this website for more documentation: http://www.agreementsonline.co.za

You must have written and well documented Standard Operating Procedures in place, for all plant and machinery, instrumentation or any other piece of equipment that an employee has to operate (e.g. training manuals and records of competence).

Also your own standard company policies for customers, list of preferred suppliers, and approved outsourced contractors.

Retention of documents: the taxman requires that you keep all financial documents (receipts, invoices, annual financials, asset registers, and bank statements) for at least 7 years. Staff records should be kept for at least 5 years of those staff that have left your employment; as well as salary registers. Company registration documents and certificates of incorporation, as well as other similar type papers should be kept indefinitely.

Nowadays, these documents can be stored on hard drives and other computer memory devices. Note that computer backup copies of critical documentation should be stored off site in case of loss of this information due to fire, theft, hard drive breakdowns, etc.

Store all your valuable documents in a fire-proof cabinet or safe.

Valuable documents could include the following:

- Title deeds;
- Partnership contracts;
- Insurance policies;
- Legal company incorporation documents and related government certificates;
- Personal confidential documents;
- Valuation certificates of your major plant and equipment;
- Annual financial statements;
- Large amounts of cash.............you would have accumulated this amount of cash if you have read and fully understood AS WELL AS IMPLEMENTED what is in this guidebook!

Disclaimers:

To somewhat protect yourself and your business against any possible litigation by you publishing to the public documents such as advertising materials and even email replies, you need to affix to the end (footer) of the documents' disclaimers. These are generally clauses that state basically your readers or public must be diligent when reading or using your published paperwork. Another way is to include the phrase "*E. & O. E.*" Which basically means that you are not responsible for any errors or omissions that you inadvertently made on documents such as invoices, quotations and estimates.

Security of documents: protect your documents (e.g. pdf files) with encrypted passwords and use electronic signatures. You can obtain an electronic signature for the protection of your signed documents by contacting organisations such as South Africa Post Office (SAPO) which uses *Docex.*

"Whatever you ardently and passionately desire, that you obtain"

----------*quote from Napoleon Bonaparte*

NOTES:

Suggest you list here your critical documents (i.e. those that you cannot afford to lose or replace):

Chapter 18

In Conclusion

There is no such thing as a "free lunch". Remember **everyone** is out to take your hard earned money away from you!

Basically there are 9 things you must do................

1. Keep 10% of whatever you earn, i.e. save 10% of your cash earnings in an account that earns COMPOUND interest.....i.e. interest earning on top of interest. Invest your earnings!
Get your business to actually pay to YOU interest (at the maximum allowable by law) on the monies (your loan account) that you have put into the business.

2. Work, no one got rich, or kept their riches, except by working (here the definition of "work" will become apparent to you, e.g. you can also "work" just by thinking and acting you are RICH!) But have a recreational break occasionally to refresh your mind, so that you can make clear and intelligent business decisions.

3. Budget! Yes, you must control your expenses! Become frugal, but not a miser; even the billionaire Donald Trump looks after his expenses.

4. Insure your business, plant and machinery, stock, etc. Yes, insurance is a must! Remember insurance is NOT an investment but does give you some sort of peace of mind. Protect yourself and your business! If you have a business partner, then insure one another's lives........consider

what would happen if you suddenly lost your partner! Would your business still function as before?

5. Buy your own premises. Yes, property is "a" good investment over a long term. But buy wisely in an area that is sure to appreciate in value. Ask questions of your local municipal planning department.

6. Save for your future (pension!), yes take out a pension or retirement annuity policy, BUT remember that this is NOT an investment, but some sort of delayed retirement salary at a much reduced value!

7. Continue to study or broaden your field of expertise! For example, if you are a plumber, then attend technical or engineering exhibitions, or something similar to keep abreast of new products, and advances in your field.

8. Be active! Make decisions and keep to them..............here you need to discipline yourself and not be **greedy** for that extra bit of money you have intentionally loaded on top of a quote or sale! Do not "rip-off" your customers, as this bad karma will come back to you!

9. BUT be cautious.............consider the consequences of your decisions!

Be awake and catch those opportunities when they come your way. You have heard the old saying: "you snooze, you lose!"

"Wealth is not his that has it, but his that enjoys it"
---------quote from Benjamin Franklin

Thank you for reading my book.

E. & O. E.

EXAMPLE 1

form BKKEEP/001-2014

Sales Receipt

Sales Receipt

Place your business name and address here		

Co. Registration No.	
VAT REG NO	
Phone number	
Fax number	

Sold To

Customer Account number	Customer Vat number	Payment Method	Date	Receipt number

Description	Qty	VAT	VAT AMT	Amount	VAT %

VAT TOTAL	
SUBTOTAL	
Total	

ref: QUICKBOOKS

100

EXAMPLE 2

Invoice

Tax Invoice

Your busines name and address goes here	Co. Registration No.
	Vat Reg No.
	Phone number
	Fax number

Invoice To:	Ship To:

Customer Order Number	Customer Vat number	Terms of Payment	Rep	Ship Date	Ship Via

Quantity	Item	Description	Price	VAT code	VAT AMT	Amount	VAT rate %

	SUBTOTAL
	VAT TOTAL
	TOTAL

ref: QUICKBOOKS

101

EXAMPLE 3

Statement

Statement

Your business name and address goes here	

Statement Date	
Phone number	
Fax number	
E-Mail	

Statement To:

Terms of payment	Due Date	Account #	Amount Due
			ZAR0.00

Date	Transaction	Amount	Balance
	Balance forward		0.00

Current	1-30 Days Past Due	31-60 Days Past Due	61-90 Days Past Due	Over 90 Days Past Due	Amount Due
0.00	0.00	0.00	0.00	0.00	ZAR0.00

ref: Quickbooks

EXAMPLE 4

form HR/001-2014

Standard Contract of Employment
Aka "Letter of Appointment"

Dear ------------------------

- I have pleasure in welcoming you to our team on a -- month contract, at ----------- per week/month as from the ----------- in the position of -----------

- Your normal working hours are from 08:00 to 17:00 (Mondays to Friday), with 30 minutes daily lunch break and a 2x 10 minutes tea break.

- Your duties will include --- and other work-related assignments. Your immediate supervisor/s will be as per our Staff Organogram, as amended from time to time.

- Please note that it is legal requirements that all factory workers are required to wear their safety and protective clothing of which the Company will supply to you at no cost.

- Your employment will be subject to our Company's Contract of Service (which includes obligations under our "Quality Management System" and our "Safety, Health & Environment Programme" of which you will be required to sign and comply with its contents.

If you have any queries, I will be pleased to discuss these with you.

Kindly confirm in writing, your acceptance of these conditions of employment.

We look forward to a long, mutually pleasant and rewarding association.

Yours sincerely

Human Resources Manager
Belts4U (Pty) Ltd

EXAMPLE 5

Form HR/004-2014

Certificate of Service

To whom it may concern

This is to certify that:

    ID Number: --

has been employed by ----------------------- (Pty) Ltd

from ------------------------------------- until--;

as--.

-- leaves our Company on his/her own accord.

----------------------------was an asset to our Company and we wish him/her everything of the best in his/her new ventures.

Human Resources Manager

Belts4U (Pty) Ltd

This is an essential document which must be given to any employee that leaves your employment whether it is by resignation, retrenchment or being fired.

EXAMPLE 6

form HR/002-2014

Job Description

Position: -----------------------------------

Incumbent/employee name: ---

Company number: ----------------

Duties:

- *(list here all the duties/work that you want this person to do)*

--

- Any other duty or assignment relevant to this type of position

----

Responsibilities:

(List here all the responsibilities that come with this position)

--

Person to report to: -----------------------------

Staff under your responsibility: ---------------------

For other duties and responsibilities not listed above, please read in conjunction with *Letter of Appointment* and the Company's *Standard Contract of Service.*

Any changes to conditions of employment and/or job description shall be by mutual consent only.

This is an essential document which must be given to each employee. Also an Organogram should be compiled of all your staff line of authority and responsibility.

EXAMPLE 7

form HR/003-2014

Leave Application Form

A: Employee to complete this part:

Employee Name: ....Company number: ....

Number of leave days requested: ....

Type of leave required: (tick the applicable box)

sick☐   maternity☐   paternity☐   study☐   unpaid☐
compassionate☐ annual☐   other☐

(Note: For sick leave a valid original doctor's certificate must accompany this form. A fax or photocopies are NOT acceptable.)

Requested date leave commences on:

Requested date of return to work:

Employee signature: .... Date: ....

-----B: Employer to complete this part:

Number of days granted: ....Number of days not granted: ....

Reason for not granting requested leave: ....

Type of leave granted: ....

Date leave commences on: ....

Date of return to work: ....

Manager/Supervisor:

Signature.......................:................................. Date: ....

Note that a copy of this completed form must be given to the employee.

EXAMPLE 8

Final Demand for Payment

Dear Sir/Madam   <u>WITHOUT PREJUDICE</u>

Re: <u>Outstanding account</u>

Please note that our terms are strictly payable on presentation of the invoice/statement.

At present (according to our records) you have the following invoices still outstanding:

Invoice:	Date:	Invoice Amount:
------------	------------------	-------------------

Our problem is, "How do we impress upon you the urgency of our request without being offensive to you?"

We would like you to know that your support has always been appreciated and we would do anything to avoid unpleasantness and to continue doing business with you/your Company.

But we need the money! How about it? **The TOTAL amount owing is R ----**

Please immediately deposit the monies into our bank account at:

Prompt payment of overdue debts will help us to stay in business today, so that we can offer our services to you again tomorrow!

Kindly complete and sign the lower portion of this notice and return to us immediately via fax/e-mail.

Your kind immediate cooperation in this urgent matter would be most welcome.

Note: If you have already paid this invoice please fax/email proof of payment, so that we may credit your account accordingly. Many Thanks.

Credit Control Manager

I, acting on behalf of.................................. (the Debtor) hereby acknowledge and pledge that we are indebted to ....,, (the Creditor) in the sum of..............being the amount owing including interest/finance charges.

Thus, done and signed at....................on the.........day of......................2014.

....

Debtor authorised signatory   Witness

EXAMPLE 9

form HR/005-2014

Grievance Procedure

A grievance is defined as any cause of dissatisfaction or feeling of injustice on the part of an employee or group of employees arising out of the work situation.

1.   OBJECTIVE
      The main purpose of implementing the procedure will be to prevent and resolve conflict in the workplace, to protect the interest of the company and the employees, and to recognise the rights of an employee or employees to appeal and to be given a fair hearing against any measure which he/she/they may consider to be unjust.

2.   INTENTION
      2.1.   The company and its employees agree that it is in their mutual interest to observe a grievance procedure by which issues arising between them can be resolved.
      2.2.   It is the intention of the company that grievances can be resolved as soon as possible and within set time limits.
      2.3.   Employees have the right to be accompanied by a representative (i.e. a fellow employee) of their choice at any stage. Both the employee and the employee's representative are free to submit a grievance without prejudice whatsoever, regarding employment conditions and without fear of victimisation.

3.   PROCEDURE
Step 1
(a)   An employee who has a grievance must first report such a grievance to his/her supervisor (first reporting level) and discuss the matter on an informal basis. The employee may be accompanied by a co-employee. In the event of the grievance not being resolved during these discussions, the employee must inform his/her supervisor that he/she wishes the matter to be treated as a formal grievance by completing a grievance form in writing.
(b)   The supervisor must, to the best of his/her ability:
       (i)   listen to the employee in private;
       (ii)   encourage the employee to express his/her grievance freely and openly; and
       (iii)   obtain all relevant facts about the grievance (distinguishing facts from opinion).
(c)   The supervisor must endeavour to resolve the grievance as speedily as possible and resolve this within, at most, three working days.
(d)   In the event of the grievance not being resolved by the supervisor, Step 2 becomes effective, and the supervisor must advise the

employee of the subsequent stages of the procedure and of the employee's right to seek the assistance of a representative.

Step 2

(a) If the employee elects to proceed with the grievance then he/she must, with the assistance of a representative, if chosen, record the relevant details on the grievance form.

(b) The signed form must be handed to the supervisor, who must record his/her findings on the grievance form and return it to the employee.

(c) If the employee is not satisfied with the outcome, he/she may proceed to Step 3.

Step 3

(a) The employee will hand the grievance form to the H.O.D (Head of Department or Manager), who shall hold an enquiry into the matter within two working days of receipt thereof.

(b) The enquiry shall be attended by the H.O.D, the supervisor, the employee and his/her representative. A record of the enquiry must be kept.

(c) The H.O.D must give his/her decision within one working day of the enquiry.

(d) The H.O.D's decision must be recorded on the grievance form and a signed copy handed to the employee.

(e) If the employee is not satisfied with the outcome, he/she may proceed to Step 4.

Step 4

(a) The employee will hand the grievance form to the CEO (Chief Executive Officer or Director or Owner) who shall hold an enquiry into the matter within two working days of receipt thereof.

(b) The CEO must give a decision within one working day of the enquiry and the CEO's decision must be recorded on the grievance form and a signed copy handed to the employee.

(c) If the employee is still not satisfied with the outcome, he/she may proceed to Step 5.

Step 5

The employee may refer the matter to the CCMA or any other similar government labour department.

GRIEVANCE FORM

Name of Aggrieved Employee	
Supervisor	
Department	

DETAILS OF GRIEVANCE

Reported verbally to Supervisor on	

FORM HANDED TO:

Supervisor	

Signature	
Date	

SUPERVISOR'S ACTION:

_____

_____
_____
_____

REFERRED TO THE H.O.D ON:

H.O.D	
Signature	
Date	
Enquiry Held on	
Findings of Enquiry	

REFERRED TO THE C.E.O ON:

C.E.O	
Signature	
Date	
Enquiry Held On	
Findings of Enquiry	

EXAMPLE 10

Form HR/006-2014

Disciplinary Code

INTRODUCTION

This document serves to provide a uniform disciplinary code and procedure for the Company to ensure that all employees are treated in a fair and consistent manner in circumstances where disciplinary action is required. It is, however, neither rigid nor inflexible and management may, at its discretion, implement less or more severe disciplinary action as and when required. It is the responsibility of management to maintain discipline at the Company and the code recognises the right of management to initiate disciplinary action against any employee where circumstances so warrant.

1.   INFRINGEMENTS, OFFENCES AND PENALTIES

The disciplinary procedure will be initiated against any employee who contravenes the disciplinary code, or who acts against the interests of the Company or who commits any social, criminal or other offence.

The disciplinary measures include a verbal warning, a written warning, a final written warning and dismissal. Punitive suspension and/or demotion may only be given as alternatives to dismissal.

2.   CUMULATIVE NATURE OF DISCIPLINARY ACTION

The Company supports the tenets of the current Labour Relations laws, and to this end implements a system of progressive discipline.

PROCEDURE

1.   In cases where, *prima facie*, it appears as if the appropriate penalty may be a dismissal, a disciplinary enquiry must be convened.

2.   The authorised officer (a member of management) must determine whether there is adequate proof to suggest that the offence has been committed before taking the appropriate disciplinary action.

3.   Other disciplinary procedures shall be less formal. No decision regarding disciplinary action will be taken without first providing the employee with the opportunity of defending himself/ herself, unless the company cannot reasonably be expected to provide this opportunity.

4.   In all cases of company discipline only in-house representation from company employees will be allowed.

The Disciplinary Enquiry

(prima facie case of dismissal)

Stage 1 - Before the Enquiry

The employee must be notified in writing of the pending disciplinary enquiry (Advice to attend a disciplinary enquiry form). The following requirements must be met:

a)   this notification must be given 48 hours before the actual hearing;

b)   the charge against the respective employee must be specified;

c)   the employee must be informed that he/ she has the right to be represented by a fellow employee; and

111

d)   the employee must be informed of his/ her right to adduce evidence and call witnesses, as well as the right to question Company evidence and cross-examine Company witnesses.

Stage 2 - The Plea and Determination of Guilt
Before a decision concerning guilt is taken:

a)   the charge must be put to the employee and he/ she must be given the opportunity of pleading guilty or not guilty;

b)   if he/ she pleads **guilty**, questions must be asked to determine whether he/ she understands the charge. If it is clear that he/ she understands the charge, the employee can be found guilty and the presiding officer can move to the third stage;

c)   if the employee pleads **not guilty**, evidence must be led and the following procedure adopted:

(i)   All the witnesses in support of the case must give evidence;

(ii)   Upon completion of evidence of each witness, the employee and his/ her representative must be given the opportunity to cross-examine the witness;

(iii)   When all the witnesses have been led, the employee must be given the opportunity to lead his/ her evidence, in person, and call witnesses, who may be cross-examined.

A decision concerning **guilt** must then be made. (The presiding officer should not look at the employee's previous record at this stage). Before making the decision, an adjournment may be requested by the presiding officer in order to consider all the information gained and apply his/ her mind to the facts. If an employee is **guilty**, proceed to stage 3. If found **not guilty**, the employee is excused and the incident may not be taken into consideration again.

Stage 3 - Penalty Consideration
A decision concerning sanction is made at this stage.

The employee should be requested to plead in mitigation, and the Company may argue in aggravation. All factors must be taken into account, including the gravity of the misconduct, length of service, previous disciplinary record, personal circumstances, and the nature of the job and the circumstances of the infringement itself. Based on all the evidence and the code, a decision regarding sanction is then made.

Stage 4 - Notification of Penalty
The employee should be given his/ her sanction in writing by the presiding officer. If it is dismissal then the reasons for dismissal must also be given.

Stage 5 - Appeal
The purpose of an appeal is to provide a dismissed employee the opportunity to redress any alleged irregularities resultant from the disciplinary enquiry.

The appeal application must be submitted to management, on the prescribed format, within three (3) days of the outcome of the disciplinary enquiry.

The person who chaired the disciplinary enquiry cannot chair the appeal hearing. It must be a different person and preferably of a more senior rank.

The manager will arrange for the convening of an appeal hearing within three (3) days of the appeal being lodged.

The appeal hearing will give consideration to the following:

(a) Incorrect findings on facts (new evidence)
(b) Procedural error.
(c) Prejudice/ bias on the part of the Chairperson.
(d) The appropriateness of the sanction imposed.

The procedure to be followed is:

(a) Evidence of the accused, witnesses and management must be led and cross-examined as necessary, depending upon the grounds of the appeal.
(b) The Chairperson may adjourn and reconvene the hearing as necessary.
(c) The Chairperson must adjourn to apply his/ her mind and upon return advise the parties of the finding in writing.
(d) The Chairperson must inform the accused of his/ her right to refer the matter further, to either the relevant Bargaining Council or the CCMA.
(e) The original copies of the appeal form, record of proceedings and the result of the appeal hearing must be handed to and kept by the manager.

Stages of Disciplinary Measures

Verbal Warning (Authourised Official)
Verbal warnings may be issued by an authorised official for minor disciplinary infringements. A written record should be kept of such warnings. Verbal warnings will be valid for 3 (three) months.

Written Warning (Authourised Official)
a) All written warnings should be recorded in duplicate and should state the date on which the offence took place, the date on which the warning was issued, the reasons for the warning and any corrective action which may be required to correct or improve performance or change behaviour.
b) Where a warning is issued the employee should be advised that failure on his/ her part to correct or improve performance or change behaviour will result in further and possibly more severe disciplinary action being taken.
c) The employee will be required to sign the warning, not as an admission of guilt, but to indicate that he/ she has received it. Should an employee refuse to sign the warning this should be noted by having a witness sign the form verifying the fact that the employee party refused to sign.
d) The warnings should also be signed by the authorised official and the employee's representative, where applicable.
e) The original copy of the warning must be kept on the employee's personal file and the duplicate handed to the employee.
f) Each written warning will be cancelled after the expiry of a period of 6 (six) months provided no similar offences are committed during that period.

113

Final Written Warning (Authourised Official)

a) When an employee has accumulated the requisite number of warnings in terms of the disciplinary code or where the nature of the offence warrants it, a final written warning may be issued.

b) A procedure notifying the employee of the charge, allowing the employee internal representation, proving the charge, allowing a defence, a decision regarding guilt and determination of the appropriate sanction must be followed.

c) When issuing a final warning, the authorised official must make it clear to the employee concerned that a final written warning is viewed seriously and that any further breach of discipline within the particular category of offence within the next six months could result in dismissal.

d) Each final written warning will be cancelled after the expiry of a period of 12 (twelve) months provided no similar offences are committed during that period.

Dismissal

a) Where an employee has accumulated the requisite number of warnings in terms of the disciplinary code or where the nature of the offence warrants it, dismissal may be considered. If dismissed, the employee must be reminded of their right to challenge the decision taken by invoking the dispute resolution procedures as per the Labour Relations Act.

b) If the nature of the offence warrants it, the employee concerned may be suspended on full pay until a disciplinary enquiry has been completed and a decision made as to the form of disciplinary action to be taken. If the employee is found guilty, the period of suspension shall be without pay.

c) The presiding officer shall decide on the appropriate disciplinary action only after investigating the incident and considering all the facts and circumstances.

d) The exact nature of the employee's offence and the decision taken by the presiding officer must be recorded on the relevant form. This form must be signed where required by the employee concerned and the presiding officer. Should an employee refuse to sign the form this should be verified by having another witness sign?

THE DISCIPLINARY CODE

CATEGORY	NATURE OF OFFENCE	DISCIPLINARY ACTION			
		FIRST OFFENCE	SECOND OFFENCE	THIRD OFFENCE	FOURTH OFFENCE
TIMEKEEPING OFFENCES	Late for work or leaving work early without good reason	Verbal Warning	Written Warning	Final Written Warning	Dismissal

	Unwarranted or unauthorised absence from place of work without good reason	Verbal Warning	Written Warning	Final Written Warning	Dismissal
	Absence – away from work for five or more working days without permission, or without good reason	Dismissal			
	Fraudulent timekeeping	Dismissal			
WORK OUTPUT OFFENCES	Poor performance (low quantity of output and unsatisfactory attitude to such performance)	Verbal Warning	Written Warning	Final Written Warning	Dismissal
	Sleeping on duty	Final Written Warning	Dismissal		
	Unacceptable work habits	Verbal Warning	Written Warning	Final Written Warning	Dismissal
	Idling, loafing or purposeless activity	Verbal Warning	Written Warning	Final Written Warning	Dismissal
	Refusal to work	Dismissal			
	Refusal to obey reasonable instructions related to work	Final Written Warning	Dismissal		
QUALITY OF WORK OFFENCES	Poor quality of and/ or not working to standards	Written Warning	Final Written Warning	Dismissal	
	Poor maintenance of vehicle/ machinery/ equipment	Final Written Warning	Dismissal		
	Wastage of material	Final Written Warning	Dismissal		
	Negligent damage to equipment, material or Company property	Final Written Warning	Dismissal		
	Malicious damage to equipment, material or Company property	Dismissal			

	Injury to others through negligence or horseplay	Final Written Warning	Dismissal		
	Disorderly behaviour	Final Written Warning	Dismissal		
SOCIAL OFFENCES	Under the influence of alcohol or intoxicating drugs at work, or reporting for duty in such a state	Counselling/ Dismissal			
	Unauthorised possession of alcohol or non-medical drugs on work premises	Counselling/ Dismissal			
	Threat of or actual physical violence/ assault	Dismissal			
	Sexual harassment	Dismissal			
	Intimidation or incitement to violence, victimisation, racial discrimination	Dismissal			
	Committing unsanitary acts	Final Written Warning	Dismissal		
ATTITUDINAL OFFENCES	Breach of employees' duty of good faith to the Company, including disclosure of confidential information, damaging the image/ reputation of the Company, injury to fellow employee's dignity/ honour/ good name, unauthorised statements to the media	Dismissal			
	Failure to wear protective clothing or equipment where supplied	Final Written Warning	Dismissal		
	Failure or refusal to carry	Final Written	Dismissal		

116

	out a reasonable and lawful instruction	Warning			
	Failure to observe security, safety and Company rules & regulations	Final Written Warning	Dismissal		
	Smoking in a "No Smoking" area	Final Written Warning	Dismissal		
	Being in an "out of bounds" area without authorisation or without good reason	Final Written Warning	Dismissal		
	Use of abusive and/ or derogatory and/ or offensive language or signs	Final Written Warning	Dismissal		
	Gross insubordination, serious disrespect, impudence or insolence	Dismissal			
	Negligence/ neglect of duties	Final Written Warning	Dismissal		
	Gross dishonesty/ fraudulent conduct	Dismissal			
	Gross negligence	Dismissal			
OTHER OFFENCES	Wilful damage to company materials, equipment, possessions or property	Dismissal			
	Unlawful possession/ wrongful use of company property	Dismissal			
	Industrial sabotage	Dismissal			
	Driving company vehicle whilst under the influence of alcohol or drugs	Dismissal			
	Driving company vehicle without	Dismissal			

117

	authority				
	Dishonesty during the course of employment	Dismissal			
	Divulgence of confidential company information	Dismissal			
	Deliberately supplying incorrect or falsified information	Dismissal			
	Excessive private use of the telephone	Verbal Warning	Written Warning	Final Written Warning	Dismissal
	Unauthorised acceptance of cash, gifts &/ or any other form of remuneration	Dismissal			
	Any other reason recognised in law as being sufficient grounds for instant dismissal	Dismissal			

DISCIPLINARY ACTION FOR OTHER MISCONDUCT

Any misconduct not specifically covered in the code will be dealt with according to the seriousness of the offence.

NOTE:

The code makes provision for progressive disciplinary actions in each category of offence. Discipline will therefore be taken progressively in each category of offence and not necessarily only in regard to a specific offence. The disciplinary action prescribed by the code may be deviated from where justified by the particular circumstances of the case. Accordingly, such action may be more severe than the prescribed guideline where aggravating circumstances exist, or less severe where mitigating circumstances exist. In certain circumstances and in the case of certain offences, dismissal even for a first offence would be appropriate.

ADVICE TO ATTEND A DISCIPLINARY ENQUIRY

(To be issued 48 hours prior to enquiry)

Name of Employee	
Date of Enquiry	
Time of Enquiry	
Place of Enquiry	

ALLEGED MISCONDUCT/ CHARGE(S) – SPECIFY:

_____

_____

You have the right to be represented/ assisted by a fellow employee/union representative (and to an interpreter) at the enquiry. Further, you have the right to call witnesses and/ or lead other evidence.

The alleged misconduct constitutes a serious breach of the policies and rules of the company and you are instructed to attend and exercise your rights at the enquiry, failing which it will proceed in your absence or without such exercise. Any unjustified failure to attend the enquiry will not be condoned by management and further disciplinary action may be taken on this ground.

Employee   **Date**

NOTE: DUPLICATE TO BE RETAINED AND THE FOLLOWING IS TO BE COMPLETED THEREON.

This notice was served on the above-mentioned employee by the undersigned at _____ hr. _____ on the ___day of_____, and the contents were clearly read and explained to the employee by the undersigned.

Signature   **Date**   **Designation**

The employee is reminded of his/her right to refer the matter to a Bargaining Council or the Commission for Conciliation, Mediation and Arbitration within 30 (thirty) days hereof.

PROCEDURE FOR CONDUCTING A DISCIPLINARY ENQUIRY
(Prima Facie Case of Dismissal)

STAGE 1: BEFORE THE ENQUIRY	
Employee to be notified in writing of the pending disciplinary enquiry The following requirements must be met: 1. Notification to be given 48 hours before the actual hearing 2. Charge(s) against the employee to be specified 3. Employee informed of right to representation by a fellow employee/ adduce evidence/ lead witnesses	

STAGE 2A: THE PLEA AND DETERMINATION OF GUILT	

Charge(s) put to the employee who must plead guilty or not guilty.
1. If he/ she pleads guilty, ensure that the charge is understood and if it is, move to stage 3
2. If the employee pleads not guilty, evidence must be led as follows:
  • Complainant's statement followed by cross-examination (if appropriate)
  • Witnesses in support of the case give evidence, followed by cross-examination
  • Employee's statement followed by cross-examination
  • Employee witnesses lead by employee, followed by cross-examination	

STAGE 2B:	
1. A decision concerning guilt must then be made (Presiding Officer to consider proven evidence on a balance of probabilities) and the Presiding Officer may adjourn in order to consider the information gained 2. If an employee is guilty, proceed to stage 3. If found not guilty, the employee is excused and the incident may not be taken into consideration again.	
EXAMINE THE ALLEGATIONS AND THE EMPLOYEE'S RESPONSE IN THE LIGHT OF:	
1. Whether or not the employee contravened a rule/ standard regulating conduct in or of relevance to the workplace; 2. Whether the rule/ standard was valid and reasonable; 3. Whether the employee was aware or could reasonably be expected to be aware of the rule/standard 4. Whether the rule/standard has been consistently applied; 5. Whether dismissal is an appropriate sanction	
STAGE 3: PENALTY CONSIDERATION	
The employee should be requested to plead in mitigation and the Presiding Officer is to take due consideration of: 1. Employee length of service 2. Previous disciplinary record 3. Whether a continued employment relationship has become intolerable due to the employee's conduct	
STAGE 4: NOTIFICATION OF PENALTY	
The employee to be notified in writing of the decision taken and the reasons for the finding. If dismissal is decided on, the employee is to be informed of his/ her right to appeal and/or refer the matter to the CCMA within 30 days of the date of dismissal.	

DISCIPLINARY ENQUIRY:
MINUTES OF PROCEEDINGS HELD ON

Name of Employee	
Presiding Officer	

Authorised Official	
Representative	

STAGE 1: PRE-ENQUIRY REQUIREMENTS
1.   Was notification given at least 48 hours prior to the actual hearing?
        Yes/ No
2.   Were the charges against the employee specified? Yes/ No
3.   Was the employee informed of his/her right to representation, lead
        evidence and witnesses? Yes/ No
4.   Has the employee been afforded a reasonable time to consult with
        his/her fellow employee/union representative? Yes/ No

STAGE 2: THE PLEA AND DETERMINATION OF GUILT

_____

_____

PART A:
Charges
1.   How does the employee plead?

Guilty	Not Guilty

        (NOTE: Do not let the employee start giving evidence or explaining
        his/ her reply to the question at this stage)
2.   If the employee pleads guilty, explain the complainant to the
        employee and satisfy yourself that he/ she understands the charge
        and intends to plead guilty.

Charge(s) Reiterated/ Explained	Employee Understands	Employee Confirms Pleading Guilty	Not Applicable

3.   Authorised Official's statement/ evidence (follow by cross-
        examination when appropriate)
        COMPLAINANT: _____

        _____

        CROSS-EXAMINATION/ QUESTIONS: _____

        _____

        _____

        _____

4.   Evidence of witnesses in support of charges

        _____

_____
_____

5.   Employee's statement/ evidence (followed by cross-examination where appropriate)
EMPLOYEE: _____

_____

_____

CROSS-EXAMINATION/ QUESTIONS: _____

_____

_____

_____

OTHER EVIDENCE SUBMITTED _____

_____

_____

6.   Evidence of witnesses of employee

_____

_____

_____

PART B:
7.   Excuse complainant and employee party.
Is there sufficient grounds/ proven evidence on a balance of probabilities in order to find the employee guilty? Yes/ No
Has the employee contravened a rule/ standard? Yes/ No
Was the rule/ standard valid and reasonable? Yes/ No
Was the employee aware/ could employee have been expected to be aware thereof? Yes/ No
Has the rule/ standard been consistently applied? Yes/ No

If Yes, list such:

STAGE 3:
1.   Call the parties back into proceedings (not the witnesses).
2.   Communicate the decision reached (i.e. Guilty/ Not Guilty) as well as the reasons for the decision.
3.   Request the employee to read in mitigation and consider issues raised. Excuse the Parties.
STAGE 4:
Contemplate appropriate sanction in the circumstances, taking factors raised in mitigation as well as aggravation and the guidelines of the disciplinary code into account. Yes/ No

Penalty imposed

Reason(s) for decision:

Advised employee in writing of findings and penalty Yes/ No

DISCIPLINARY ACTION
(Short of Dismissal)

Name of Employee	
Name of Authorised Official	
Date of this Interview	

DESCRIBE THE SITUATION AND REVIEW PREVIOUS DISCUSSIONS
Remember –
- be specific
- provide a concise review of:
- previous discussions
- agreed-upon actions
- actions actually taken
- maintain or enhance self esteem

_____

_____

_____

_____

_____

_____

_____

_____

_____

_____

_____

_____

_____

ASK FOR REASONS FOR THE BEHAVIOUR

Remember –
- use open-ended questions
- ask for help in solving the problem
- maintain or enhance self esteem

123

_____

_____

_____

_____

DISCUSS CAUSES OF THE PROBLEM

Remember –
- listen attentively
- identify feelings
- summarise reasons
- listen and respond with empathy

_____

_____

_____

_____

_____

_____

_____

_____

INDICATE WHAT ACTION YOU MUST TAKE AND WHY
Remember –
- refer to disciplinary code
- be specific in describing:
- measures to be taken
- why necessary
- be non-threatening
- maintain or enhance self esteem
- listen and respond with empathy

ACTION		REASONS FOR ACTION
	Verbal Warning	

124

Written Warning	
Final Written Warning	
Referred to a Disciplinary Hearing	

AGREE ON SPECIFIC ACTION AND FOLLOW-UP DATE

Remember –

- seek and use employee's ideas, if possible
- develop specific action plan
- maintain or enhance self esteem
- ask for help in solving the problem

Date and Time of follow-up Interview		
SIGNED BY:		
Authorised Official		Date:

Employee		Date:
Representative		Date:
Copies To	* Employee * Supervisor Concerned * Personnel Department for employee file	

NOTIFICATION OF DISMISSAL
(Copy placed in employee's file)

Name of Employee	
Date of Enquiry	
Charge	
Finding	
Penalty	

_____

_____

_____

_____

Presiding Officer	/ / Date

Original received by me.

Employee	/ / Date

Fellow Employee	/ / Date

The employee is reminded of his/ her right to refer the matter to a Bargaining Council or the Commission for Conciliation, Mediation and Arbitration within 30 (thirty) days hereof.

DISCIPLINARY APPEAL FORM

Name of Employee	

Date	
Position and Department	
Appeal Submitted By	
Position (Employee/ Representative)	

APPEAL AGAINST DISMISSAL

GROUNDS FOR APPEAL:

1.   Lack of Jurisdiction _____

_____

_____

2.   Procedural Irregularity _____

_____

_____

3.   Finding on facts (do you have any new evidence to adduce?) _____

_____

_____

4.   Penalty _____

_____

_____

_____   ____/____/____
Signature of Appellant   Date

_____   ____/____/____
Signature of Representative   Date

THE APPEAL HEARING

Chairperson:

Job title: _____

Department: _____

Date: _____

Appellant: _____

Representatives:

Witnesses: _____

Chairperson to read reasons for Appeal.
Statement of case by appellant (written statement to be submitted)

_____

_____

_____

_____

_____

_____

_____

_____Evidence of persons

present to be heard and cross-examined by Chairperson and recorded as

necessary.

_____

_____

_____

_____Chairperson to determine:

1.1.   Uphold disciplinary enquiry finding, as well as penalty
        imposed.

1.2.   Uphold disciplinary enquiry finding, but impose different
        penalty

1.3.   Overturn disciplinary enquiry finding. Employee exonerated.

2. Chairperson to communicate decision.

RESULT OF APPEAL HEARING:

At an appeal hearing convened on the _____ day of _____

2014, at _____hr._____ (time) and based on the evidence presented,

the findings of the Chairperson are:

(Place an X in the appropriate box)
1. Uphold the disciplinary enquiry finding and penalty.   [   ]
2. Uphold the disciplinary enquiry finding, but no penalty   [   ]
3. Overturn disciplinary enquiry finding, employee exonerated   [   ]
Reasons for decision:

128

_____
_____
_____
_____

_____   _____

(Chairperson Signature)   (Employee Signature)

_____
_____   -

(Chairperson Job Title)   (Date)

129

"There are no secrets to success. It is the result of preparation, hard work, and learning from failure"

----------quote from Colin Powell

EXAMPLE 11

form HR/007-2014

Interviewer's Guide for Job Applicants

Before an interview, check the job applicant out on social media, such as Facebook.

Was the applicant on time for the interview? Was he/she smartly dressed and well groomed? Did he/she have a pleasant and friendly appearance? Could he/she speak good English? If any negative answers, then do not employ!

Questions to ask the job applicant:

1.   What are your interests? How do you spend your free time?
Their hobbies, sports, reading material, family time. Basically get them to talk about themselves. Do their answers collaborate what you found on their Facebook? Are they honest, trustworthy and have integrity?

2.   What are your qualifications (if any are mandatory for the vacancy)?
He/she must not answer "It's in my CV that I sent you" otherwise this would indicate insubordination. Are they qualified, or over qualified, for the job vacancy? Does the qualification match somewhat the job description?

3.   Do you have your own car and a current driver's license (if a requirement for the vacancy)?
If this was an advertised requirement for the vacancy and their answer is negative to both questions, then they were not honest in their application and have no integrity.........DO NOT EMPLOY THIS APPLICANT!

4.   Why did you decide to study for this qualification or follow this career path?
Note as to whether their remarks correlate with their interests and their work experiences.

5.   Do you want to study further and why?
This should indicate their career aspirations. Note whether they just answer yes because they think that that is the correct answer. Note if they are genuine in their replies.

6.   What are your work related strengths?
They must verbally list their greatest strengths and give specific examples that illustrate each attribute. How would their skills benefit the Company? So called "valued traits" such as a great achiever, intelligent, hardworking, good communicator with people, dedicated to job, etc. are of no consequence as every applicant advocates these personal traits.

7.   What are your weaknesses?
Try and determine if they are genuine in their reply; get them to state what areas they feel they are not competent or are inadequate.

8.   What are your work experiences and skills?
Get them to verbally talk about work experiences and why they left their previous employers. Ask where they would like to work and why; if they reply that they would like to work for you (a very common reply), then they are just telling you what you want to hear and therefore would not be suitable as an honest employee.

9.   Why should we hire you?
Try and determine if they are genuine in this reply. They must give some indication as to why they would be of true benefit to the business.

10.   Are you able to work overtime and weekends if necessary (if necessary for the vacancy)?
Try and determine if they are genuine in their reply; ensure that they do not have any religious beliefs, family commitments, transport problems or any other possible reasons as to not be able to work when requested by their superior.

11.   Why do you want to leave your current employer?
If they speak badly of their previous employer/s then they probably would not be loyal employees to any new employer. If the answer is for more money, then they would probably immediately "jump" to the next job offer.........DO NOT EMPLOY THIS APPLICANT!

12.   Why have you changed jobs so frequently?
Try and determine if they are genuine in their reply. A reasonable guideline for an uncommitted employee is where he/she has had about one job every year on average, if so, then ....DO NOT EMPLOY THIS APPLICANT!

13.   Why do you want to work here?

Have they researched the Company, e.g. on the internet or checked the Company's website? If answer is no, then they are not really interested in a career or long term employment with your business.........DO NOT EMPLOY THIS APPLICANT!

14.   Would you be interested in any other type of position in our Company?
Try and determine if they have not yet decided in a career path or have aspirations for promotion. Is he/she ambitious?

15.   What are your greatest accomplishments in life?
Check to see if applicant has confidence in himself/herself; determine if the applicant would be a suitable leader; or just an employee who wants to work 8 to 5 job?

16.   What have you done that shows initiative?
Try and determine if they are genuine in their reply. Has applicant done any work at home, on the odd occasions, for current or past employers?

17.   Can you work under stress and pressure and explain how you handle it?
Try and determine if they are genuine in their reply. In most cases an applicant would reply yes, but get them to give some examples of past experiences.

18.   What are your Career Aspirations? Where do you see yourself in 3 to 5 years' time?
Try and determine if they are genuine in their reply. If their reply is other than continuous employment with the Company, then.........DO NOT EMPLOY THIS APPLICANT!

19.   What salary are you worth, and why?
Try and determine if they are genuine in their reply. If their expectations are far too optimistic and unrealistic, then ....DO NOT EMPLOY THIS APPLICANT!

20.   What salary are you getting now?
Ask for copy of their latest pay slip. If their present salary is more than 10% then what is offered for the vacancy, then they are just "jumping jobs".........DO NOT EMPLOY THIS APPLICANT!
Do not offer a starting salary at this stage, but you can advise applicant (if they passed all the above criteria) what your business has to offer in

terms of performance bonuses, regular salary increases, quick promotions, job satisfaction, flexi time, etc.

At end of interview, advise the applicant that you will contact them after you have interviewed the other applicants.

INDEX

A

B

C

D

E

F

funding · 22

M

margin · 45
market place · 70
market research · 82, 85
Mission Statement · 24

N

name · 4, 6, 27, 28, 75, 96, 110
National B-BBEE Registry · viii
net income · 45
net profit after tax · 45
newsletters · 75, 76

O

Organisational Chart · 65
Organogram · 65
output vat · 59, 60

P

Pareto Principle · viii
Partnerships · 5
passing trade · 31
Paterson Grading System · 65
payment due date · 36
Peter's Principle · 64
plant & machinery · 62
preferred suppliers · viii, 98
premises · 13, 17, 30, 31, 94, 103
Prescription Act · 56
pricing · 58
procurement of suppliers · viii
Profit & Loss Statement · 39, 41
profit margin before tax · 45
Profitability · 43
pro-forma invoice · 37
Proprietary Limited Companies (Pty) Ltd · 5
Public Limited Companies (Ltd) · 4
Public Relations · 79

R

record periods · 99
registration · 5, 10, 12, 23, 28, 36, 99
registration numbers · 13
Remittance Advice · 37
rent · 31, 32

W

website · 6, 13, 27, 62, 74, 75, 77

Z

zero rated vat · 36

NOTES

NOTES

NOTES